THE
AFTERLIFE
SURVEY

THE
AFTERLIFE
SURVEY

A Rabbi, a CEO, a Dog Walker, and
Others on the Universal Question—What Comes Next?

MAUREEN MILLIKEN

Avon, Massachusetts

Published by
Adams Media, a division of F+W Media, Inc.
57 Littlefield Street, Avon, MA 02322. U.S.A.
www.adamsmedia.com

ISBN 10: 1-4405-1254-X
ISBN 13: 978-1-4405-1254-4
eISBN 10: 1-4405-3137-4
eISBN 13: 978-1-4405-3137-8

Printed in the United States of America.

10 9 8 7 6 5 4 3 2 1

Library of Congress Cataloging-in-Publication Data
is available from the publisher.

This book is available at quantity discounts for bulk purchases.
For information, please call 1-800-289-0963.

DEDICATION

To Mark Henderson (August 19, 1958–July 24, 2011).

Mark embraced this project from day one with patience, enthusiasm, and grace, and showed, above all, that whatever may or may not await, it's how a person tackles the here and now that says everything that needs to be said.

ACKNOWLEDGMENTS

I would like to thank all the respondents to our survey, who, to a person, openly shared some of their deepest beliefs with very little prompting, cajoling, or badgering. Their profiles appear in this book, and they're a group of very special people. I'd particularly like to thank those who stepped in without a lot of time left and were incredibly helpful and forthcoming, particularly John Bear Mitchell and John Griffin. A very special thanks to Mark Henderson, who certainly didn't have to do it, but wanted to. I'd also like to thank Ashleen O'Gaea, Arin Murphy-Hiscock, Paldrom Collins, Kendra Vaughn Hovey, and particularly Ilene Schneider, Ken Shouler, and Andy Gurevich, for all their help and quick responses to every "one last final question." Thank you, too, to the crew at Adams Media, particularly Paula Munier, for thinking of me. While he had nothing to do with this book, I owe Joe Owen a huge debt of gratitude for making what could have been a nightmare as smooth as possible, which was a tremendous help to getting it done and meeting my deadline. And to my family, for all the patience, support, for hooking me up with some of the best interviews and always lending an ear.

CONTENTS

Introduction: What We Believe

Recent polls say about three-quarters of Americans believe in an afterlife, though belief in an actual heaven and hell is falling by the wayside. The Afterlife Survey respondents agreed. The average American growing up in the latter half of the twentieth century, no matter what his or her religion, most likely believed that if you're good you'll go to heaven, and if you're bad you'll go to hell. Most Americans belonged to some sort of organized religion. They believed its doctrine without question, and it formed the backbone of their lives. This belief in heaven and hell, and how to get there, was the basis for most religious belief.

Or at least that's what most of us thought.

In recent years, growing numbers of Americans have rejected organized religion. In fact, according to the Pew Forum U.S. Religious Landscape Survey results released in 2008, nearly 28 percent of Americans have left the religion in which they were raised. Some 16 percent say they are not affiliated with any organized religion at all. That's more than double the number of people who say they weren't affiliated with a religion as children. So the assumption would be that if people are rejecting organized religion, they're also rejecting one of its most basic truths: belief in the eternal soul.

But, most of us—74 percent, according to that same Pew study—believe in an afterlife. Some surveys show that number to be even higher. But even if the Pew numbers are low, that's up from 69 percent in 1973. And yet fewer Americans than ever before believe there is a hell—only 59 percent, according to the Pew numbers. Of those who *don't* believe in God—the 12 percent of Americans who are atheists—more than one in ten still believe there is an afterlife.

However, one of the biggest findings of that Pew report is that most people don't see the afterlife as the traditional "heaven." They see it as more of an amorphous, indefinable state of being. What's more, most people are also willing to accept others' view that the afterlife may be different from what they themselves believe.

The surveys that are the foundation of this book reflect the same truth. We talked to people from a wide slice of life: a CEO, teachers, a sheet-metal worker, a dog walker, a sportswriter, a 78-year-old Catholic priest, and a 26-year-old executive assistant. We surveyed a former Buddhist nun, a rabbi, and two Wiccan priestesses. We talked to a funeral director who faces issues of life and death every day.

We talked to an atheist engineer and business owner who spent sixteen weeks in the hospital, most of it paralyzed and unable to breathe, forced to confront his own mortality.

We talked to a former Methodist minister, now an atheist, who has been told there is nothing more that can be done for his terminal cancer.

Many of these people believe there is an afterlife; some of them don't. But almost all believe there is some force in the human spirit that makes life worth living—and that the life we live on earth is just as important as what may or may not come after.

AN UNSCIENTIFIC SAMPLING

The Afterlife Survey is not based on a long-term accumulation of data from a particular demographic, but rather a cross-section sampling at this moment in time of people from different religious and cultural backgrounds, clergy, and experts in their fields. The questions were simple: What do you believe? And why? Those questioned were told there were no wrong answers.

The answers were wildly diverse—as varied as the people who were asked—but there were similar themes that ran through almost every answer.

In many cases, we just sat back and let our responders tell their stories, because so many of them had good stories to tell. One thing we learned was that the biggest certainty for almost everyone in this survey is that we really can't know what awaits us.

"I don't subscribe to the view there's an ascension into the clouds in the blue sky," said the Reverend Damian Milliken, 78, a Catholic priest and the uncle of the author. "We just can't know. St. Paul said it succinctly: 'No eye has seen, no ear has heard, no mind has conceived what God has prepared for those who love him.'"

Elizabeth Daniels, 26, of Fairfax, Virginia, works as an executive assistant/officer manager and was raised in a fundamentalist Southern Christian environment. She now considers herself an agnostic—someone who acknowledges that the existence of a supreme being can't be known—but had a surprisingly similar view to Father Milliken's.

"I believed in heaven and hell when I was a young child, and I believed in it in that silly way children do—most literally. I pictured clouds and fire, a red man and a white man with a beard and silk robes." But now, "To some extent, perhaps I do believe in an afterlife, because I am not entirely willing to say there's absolutely no such thing."

A New Hampshire newspaper editor with a master's degree in counseling, Matt McSorley, 42, believes in the traditional heaven and hell. A devout Catholic, he said his skeptical side raises questions from time to time, but if pressed, he's still in the heaven/hell camp.

Scott Moulton, 47, an investment services manager for a finance company, believes the universe is too vast to comprehend with the mind. "As I move farther and farther away from a traditional belief in heaven and hell, I have moved towards a belief in the concept that the universe itself may be alive and we may be but a subset of a much larger consciousness."

Rabbi Ilene Schneider, 62, of New Jersey, said, "Sometimes, I think that whatever someone believes about the afterlife is what they will experience. It's nice to think that someone like bin Laden, who I am sure had a deep faith that Allah would reward him for his 'martyrdom,' is now realizing Allah disagrees." But the emphasis is on "nice to think."

Poet Billy Collins, 70, of New York, who was raised in a strict Catholic home, said, "My most optimistic fantasy, which I expressed in a poem called 'The Afterlife,' is that everyone goes to the afterlife they imagined. You get what you envisioned, for better or worse. Personally, I think that hell would be stuck inside your own mind for eternity, whereas heaven would be annihilation." The former U.S. poet laureate admitted, though, "The question was long ago placed in a file labeled 'WHO KNOWS?'"

Wiccan priestess Ashleen O'Gaea said, "The broadest way I can put it is that our souls are carried by the Goddess's unconditional love to the Summerland—known by various names, including the Land of Youth—where we have an opportunity to learn from the joys and challenges of the life just lived before the God guides us back to another incarnation."

April McLeod, 45, a dog sitter who was raised by fundamentalist Christians, said, "To me, God represented love, and as the years went on I started to doubt that he could be so cruel to those who chose not to follow his path to the letter."

So . . . most of those interviewed for this survey have thought about the afterlife, no matter what it means to them, and most admit they can't really say for sure—because who can?

But they think about it anyway; we all do. If we didn't, as poet Collins points out, "We'd be hamsters."

Who Responded?
Meet the Afterlife Survey

We surveyed people from all walks of life and backgrounds to find out their views on the afterlife. Some of them not only answered surveys but also contributed expert opinions (they are noted with an *). Meet the survey respondents who provided their in-depth viewpoints:

Ian M. Clark, 37, Loudon, New Hampshire, a newspaper sportswriter and the author of several science fiction/fantasy books, most recently *Prophecy of Shadows* and *Plains of the Past*.

Afterlife quote: "I think experience and living in the world and realizing that there are so many things we don't understand about our own existence and brains has caused my view to fluctuate over time."

Billy Collins, 70, Somers, New York, poet laureate of the United States from 2001 to 2003, whose poems include "The Afterlife." Professor of English at Lehman College of City University of New York.

Afterlife quote: "The question was long ago placed in a file I labeled 'WHO KNOWS?' My most optimistic fantasy, which I expressed in a poem called "The Afterlife," is that everyone goes to the afterlife they imagined. You get what you envisioned, for better or worse. Personally, I think that hell would be stuck inside your own mind for eternity, whereas heaven would be annihilation."

*Paldrom Collins, 59, Walnut Creek, California, former Buddhist nun and counselor for people with sex addictions. She and her husband, George, have written a book on the topic, *A Couple's Guide to Sexual Addiction: A Step-by-Step Plan to Rebuild Trust & Restore Intimacy*.

Afterlife quote: "I think the fundamental question of 'Why am I here, what does my life mean?' brings with it questions about what happens after death. I'm not sure how it is possible to experience a death and not wonder, 'What happened? Where did that being go?' It matters because it is a mystery. It matters because it matters to us. Cyclical logic, yes. But true. I think we naturally seek to understand that which we don't understand."

Elizabeth Daniels, 26, Fairfax, Virginia, executive assistant/office manager for the senior vice president of contracts for a major corporation.

Afterlife quote: "I think that humanity has created ideas of God, the devil, heaven, hell, reincarnation and an afterlife, because people are afraid to admit that they do not and cannot factually know what happens after death, and they need some strong force on which to blame the daily occurrences of life. People want to think that their enemies will later on be punished after death and that their loved ones will never, ever leave them, even after their body dies on earth."

Hamid Faizid, 52, Laurel, Maryland, adult education teacher.

Afterlife quote: "After we die, we go from the grave to judgment day. We are asked questions about God and if we answer correctly, the doors of paradise are opened. If not, we are punished."

Caren Gittleman, 55, Farmington Hills, Michigan, freelance writer who blogs at *http://opcatchat.blogspot.com* and *http://dakotasden.wordpress.com.*

Afterlife quote: "Death is one of the few things we have no control of. Everyone whether they admit it or not wonders what really happens. None of us have answers because nobody knows. That is what frightens so many of us."

Barbara Grandberg, 60, Somerville, Massachusetts, retired teacher.

Afterlife quote: "We fear death, so thinking that there is an afterlife makes it easier to accept."

Larry Hausner, 70, Santa Ana, California, semi-retired CEO of the home-goods company he founded. Recently wrote a book based on his hardscrabble upbringing in Omaha, *Butter 'n Nuts.*

Afterlife quote: "I definitely believe that there is a heaven. It's difficult to believe that someone could be put into hell forever, but then I think about someone like Hitler, and have no clue where else he could have gone."

Michael Hawkins, 26, Augusta, Maine, college student, majoring in biology, and an overnight rehab counselor. Blogs at *http://forthesakeofscience.com.*

Afterlife quote: "Once I die that is the end of me. I do not continue to think or believe or feel or do anything else characteristic of life. The basis of my life is my genes and environment working in concert to produce a functional biological organism; the root of my humanity is exposed through the brain. Once the brain ends, and certainly once all the biology of my being ends, there is nothing. It will be remarkably similar to the time prior to my existence. I just won't know it."

Mark Henderson, 53, Milford, New Hampshire, college counselor and former minister, hospital chaplain, and counselor.

Afterlife quote: "[Realizing there is no afterlife] was such a freeing thing, all of a sudden now, this life was as precious as it seemed. Almost like everything in life was kind of turned up a notch or two. Everything seemed kind of beautiful and horrific to me, because everything was real and our relationship to it drives the meaning. . . . We've got life before us and what we do with it is what life means to us. It's pretty engaging, and for me it's more than enough."

Brian McHugh, 32, Manchester, New Hampshire, funeral director.

Afterlife quote: "Death is the ultimate equalizer. Regardless how successful we are here on earth or how much money we have accumulated, we cannot buy our way out of death. . . . Believing that life not only continues, but is enhanced after death can be a great comfort and support for grieving people. I firmly believe that if more choices made here on earth were influenced by the prospect of entering a glorious afterlife, many of our societal ills would be eliminated."

April McLeod, 45, Derry, New Hampshire, dog sitter, blogs at *http://theteacherspets.blogspot.com*.

Afterlife quote: "I do not believe God wants to make it difficult for anyone to get into heaven because I believe God is a God of love and not of judgment."

Matt McSorley, 42, Litchfield, New Hampshire, newspaper editor.

Afterlife quote: "There's no question more personal than the fate of our own existence. And since we on this mortal coil are unlikely ever to have our beliefs confirmed, this question will probably stay with humanity evermore."

The Reverend Damian Milliken, 78, Lushoto, Tanzania, Catholic priest and founder of Saint Mary's Mazinde Juu school for girls in Tanzania. Recently published a book of his letters from Africa, *African Pilgrimage, Volume I.* Afterlife quote: "I don't think there's any suffering after death. God is merciful, and no one is so bad that they are going to be suffering eternally."

Catherine Mills, 84, Hallowell, Maine, retired research assistant at Alzheimer's Research Center, Rush University Medical Center, Chicago. Afterlife quote: "I think a person who suffers in this life is already atoning for any sins and that limbo could well be here on earth before we die."

*John Bear Mitchell, 43, Old Town, Maine, a citizen of the Penobscot tribe, director of Wabanaki Center outreach and student development coordinator for the University of Maine System, Native American waiver coordinator, and lecturer in Wabanaki studies. Afterlife quote: "I was told that hell was full of fire but as a child who had been surrounded by traditional Native American ceremonies, I was always taught the fire is good—it keeps us warm and cooks our food. This made me question that idea of hell. . . ."

Scott Moulton, 47, Concord, New Hampshire, investment services manager. Afterlife quote: "As I move farther and farther away from a traditional belief in heaven and hell, I have moved towards a belief in the concept that the universe itself may be alive and we may be but a subset of a much larger consciousness."

*Arin Murphy-Hiscock, 40, Montreal, Quebec, a third-degree Wiccan high priestess, as well as a freelance writer, editor, and author with four books to her credit, including *Power Spellcraft for Life, Solitary Wicca for Life, The Way of the Green Witch,* and the upcoming *Birds: a Spiritual Field Guide.* She is also an editor of the anthology *Out of the Broom Closet.*

Afterlife quote: "I expect there to be a continuing cycle of existence in some form, but I think to make an assumption about what it will be would be limiting. I find the concept of the Summerland, a place/time where my spirit can reflect upon its experiences and the lessons it has learned before beginning its next cycle of existence, to be a very open one and I am comfortable with that."

*Ashleen O'Gaea, Tucson, Arizona, writer, editor, and Wiccan priestess. Author of *Family Wicca, Raising Witches, Celebrating the Seasons of Life*: *Samhain to Ostara, Celebrating the Seasons of Life*: *Beltane to Mabon, The Portable Spell Book, Enchantment Encumbered, The Green Boy, The Flower Bride,* and *Maiden, Vampire, Crone,* and *In the Service of Life: a Wiccan Perspective on Death.* She also writes a regular column in the magazine *Witches & Pagans.*

Afterlife quote: "I trust in the process of life–death–rebirth because I see it taking place all around me, all the time. I can't say from memory, but I expect it to be awesome and wonderful, and that it will be one of those, 'Oh, well, of course!' experiences."

John Reed, 42, Milton, Massachusetts, high school English teacher.

Afterlife quote: "Physically, I think you just die. I've always imagined it like the light in the old TV tube, how the picture just reduced to that tiny white spot, then it blinked out. I'm afraid of that blinking, but it's what I think happens."

Jim Robidoux, 52, Manchester, New Hampshire, sheet-metal worker.

Afterlife quote: "I believe what the Bible teaches, we will all be raised, some to eternal life, some to judgment that will be horrifying."

Anna Rossi, 75, Portland, Maine, part-time bookseller.

Afterlife quote: "My father died when I was a child. He was not a churchgoer but was a good and generous person. I remember thinking at the time that there was no way he wasn't going to heaven. That may have been the beginning of my thinking that it is not all black and white."

Martin Scattergood, 53, Dusseldorf, Germany, engineer/company owner who recently wrote a book about his experience with Guillain-Barré syndrome, called *Drowning in a Sea of Air*.

Afterlife quote: "I believe that death is finality. Therefore, we should focus on living and enjoy life."

*Ilene Schneider, 62, Marlton, New Jersey, rabbi and hospice coordinator. She has authored *Talk Dirty Yiddish: Beyond Drek* and *Chanukah Guilt*.

Afterlife quote: "Rationally, I believe when you're dead, you're dead. But emotionally, it is comforting to think this life isn't all there is. Sometimes, I think that whatever someone believes about the afterlife is what they will experience. It's nice to think that someone like bin Laden, who I am sure had a deep faith that Allah would reward him for his 'martyrdom,' is now realizing Allah disagrees."

*Ken Shouler, PhD, professor of philosophy and religion, County College of Morris, New Jersey. He has written dozens of articles and several books, including *The Everything® Guide to Understanding Philosophy, The Everything® Hinduism Book* and *The Everything® World's Religions Book.*

Afterlife quote: "There is no afterlife, since neither the evidence of the senses nor that of the intellect supports it. Camus said life was absurd, in the sense that we are here, we die and that's it. We give it meaning without projects and pursuits. We had better get on with those, since nothing follows."

Rhonda St. James, 49, Warner, New Hampshire, compliance manager for a securities broker/dealer.

Afterlife quote: "I was raised a Catholic but began rejecting most of the teachings of the Catholic faith once I began to think for myself. The more I questioned, the more that I concluded that the tenets of nearly all organized religions served the various institutions and rarely, if ever, served the faithful. It definitely caused me to question the Catholic teachings regarding the afterlife. It seemed a little convenient to believe that one could live a reprehensible life and confess at the eleventh hour and take the express elevator to Heaven. It seemed to defy logic, let alone credibility."

*Kendra Vaughn Hovey, 43, Duxbury, Massachusetts, a metaphysician, author, and freelance copy editor, is the author of *Handfasting: A Pagan Guide to Commitment Rituals* and was an editor for the anthology *Out of the Broom Closet*. Find her at *www.kvhovey .com*.

Afterlife quote: "I personally believe that God is energy or spirit. As such we live by the laws of natural order that govern the universe and never change (e.g., gravity). Knowing God as energy, there is no doubt in my mind that when I die, my spirit will unite with the spirit of God and I will be at peace and at rest."

PART ONE

Everything You Wanted to Know about the Afterlife but Were Afraid to Ask

Ever since man first started drawing pictures on the walls of caves, there's been evidence that people believed in an afterlife. The ancient Greeks, Romans, and Egyptians believed it. The Aztecs and Mayans did, too. So did those who populated North America 10,000 years ago. Their beliefs evolved into much of what we believe today. But what did people believe back then? What do traditional religions, native cultures, and nontraditional belief systems embrace? And how does all that fit in with what our survey responders believe? The first half of our book takes a look at the evolution of afterlife belief and its impact on people today.

CHAPTER ONE

WHAT HAPPENS WHEN YOU DIE?

Humankind has always believed in some sort of afterlife, from the ancient Egyptians and Mayans to the present day. Some of those beliefs have a lot in common, while others are wildly divergent, depending on the culture and people. Many of those beliefs still have an impact on what people believe today.

Ever since humans have had life, it seems, they started thinking about what would happen once they were dead. It didn't start with organized religion, Lazarus, or Jesus rising from the dead. Anthropological evidence shows that even the Neanderthals, more than 100,000 years ago, had rites that were performed at death, possibly as a way to ease the way into the afterlife.

The ancient Greeks and Romans, Aztecs, Egyptians, Chinese, Native Americans—every ancient society had a belief. Or a variety of beliefs.

Some were consumed with it.

And most of those beliefs, no matter what form a person took after he or she died or where the afterlife was, seemed to hinge on the fact that how well behaved a person was in life had a lot to do with the destination.

As people's thinking evolved and organized religion took hold, concepts of the afterlife began to have more structure, and the ideas of heaven and hell became the cornerstones of many of these beliefs. But even those groups that didn't consider heaven and hell part of the afterlife had one thing in common: if you wanted a good afterlife, you had to earn it here on earth.

"I could pull out a sermon from twenty-five years ago where I go through the reasons why it's not accurate for Christians to talk about 'an' afterlife, since there are so many references to so many different ideas in the tradition from which Christianity has arisen," said Mark Henderson, 53, of New Hampshire, a former Methodist minister. "Over the years, I came to experience, quite vividly, how the desire for a religious definition of an afterlife came from all the basic psychological fears that one would expect."

PRE-CHRISTIAN VIEWS OF THE AFTERLIFE

It didn't take Christianity and the promise of the heaven in which many modern-day people grew up believing to solidify afterlife beliefs. Ancient civilizations had very clear, and sometimes very specific, views on what comprised an afterlife. Despite the fact that these cultures spanned thousands of miles, and in some cases thousands of years, their beliefs had a lot in common. Each also had its own special twist.

The Ancient Egyptians

Ancient Egyptians made a fine art out of it, and the pyramids they built for their dead, some more than 4,000 years ago, are today among the biggest tourist attractions in the world. And they didn't limit it just to humans—cats and dogs also went to the tombs, mummified, with their masters.

Egyptians believed that once you died, you took a journey with Ra, the sun god, from whom all life came. He captained two ships—the morning ship and the evening ship, or *Mesektet*. The *Mesektet*'s destination was the underworld, and that's where Egyptians went when they died. In fact, they spent their entire lives preparing for the trip.

They believed life after death would be similar to that here on earth, so the body had to be intact for the soul to live—hence mummification and the pyramids. Not only did the body have to be intact, it had to be sustained, so gifts were frequently left with the dead.

Ancient Greece and Rome

The ancient Greeks had a pretty scary view of what happened once they died. Hades awaited across the river Styx. If you were good, you ended up in the Elysian Fields. Those who were bad, in the best case, became slight, insubstantial versions of their former selves. Those who were really bad were tortured, like poor Sisyphus, who had to roll a boulder up a hill over and over again, never quite getting to the top.

> **BAD FATE MAKES GOOD WORD**
>
> Tantalus not only stole from Zeus and revealed the gods' secrets but also cut up Zeus' son, boiled him, and then served him up for dinner to the gods. As punishment, Tantalus was sent to the darkest corner of the underworld and forced to be forever hungry, with food just out of reach. Not good for him, but great for our modern vocabulary: his fate gave us the word tantalize.

The Romans' beliefs were similar to those of the Greeks, with a lot of gods traveling back and forth to the underworld—which was ruled by Pluto, in Roman mythology—and being punished or rewarded for their deeds.

Mayan and Aztec Beliefs

Mayan and Aztec people and their cultures flourished around 2,000 years ago. Like the Greeks and Romans, they, too, were polytheistic: they believed in many gods. And, like the Greeks and Romans, the Mayans had an afterlife that included a journey down a river to an underworld. It was a dark, unpleasant place ruled by a jaguar. And almost everyone went there.

Not many people went to heaven, Tamoanchan. It was ruled by gods, and the only way to get there was to be sacrificed. As with the Ancient Egyptians, everyone who died brought some luggage on the journey, with provisions for themselves and gifts for the gods.

Eastern Beliefs

Many Eastern beliefs center around reincarnation. A person has been here before, and they'll be here again. What you come back as depends on how you behaved the last time you were here. And some of these beliefs also seek to break that cycle.

As with most other afterlife beliefs, reincarnation stresses that earthly behavior determines your fate after you're dead. In addition, like many other religious belief systems that were in place before Christianity, most ancient Eastern beliefs were polytheistic—they didn't center around one all-powerful god, but espoused a number of gods who helped guide those on earth.

Krishna was the closest thing to the one-god idea. In the Hindu scripture the Bhagavad Gita, Krishna said, "I am the source of all material and spiritual worlds. Everything emanates from me." Buddha himself derived from Krishna, and Hindu, Buddhist, and Jainist afterlife beliefs are anchored in reincarnation and karma.

Meanwhile, in China, as early as the fifth millennium B.C., people took part in elaborate death rituals. By the first millennium B.C.,

Confucius was telling his followers that the afterlife was beyond humans' ability to understand, and that the most important thing was to lead a virtuous and kind life. He is said to have told his followers, "To be able to practice five things everywhere under heaven constitutes perfect virtue. They are gravity, generosity of soul, sincerity, earnestness and kindness."

A SINGULAR GOD

Shangdi, who was believed to be the supreme being during the Han dynasty in China, first came into belief around 2000 b.c. This is believed to be one of the first references to a single god and sets it apart from the pantheistic beliefs of other cultures.

Indigenous Peoples' Beliefs

Native Americans and people from many other aboriginal cultures closely tied to nature and earth believe that the world that awaits after death is intricately tied to that of the living.

But all Native American beliefs can't be lumped under one category, cautions John Bear Mitchell, 43, a citizen of the Penobscot tribe in Maine and a lecturer at the University of Maine.

"I think far too often it is popular for nonknowing people to assume that Native Americans have many gods, when in fact we have one god and many spirits—for example, spirits of the land, of the wind, of the water, of the trees, of the animals etc., etc.," he said. "Because of popular media, our cultural beliefs have been grouped and categorized as if all Native Americans have the exact same religious/spiritual beliefs—that is a misrepresentation."

Over the centuries, many Native Americans have become Christians or have embraced other religions and beliefs, but they also still hold their basic cultural beliefs in many ways.

African tribes also have had similar beliefs, and some of these evolved into Islam, which is now the second biggest religion in the world, after Christianity.

Jewish Belief

Jews believe that every person has a *neshamah*—a soul. When a person dies, the soul returns to where it first came from, only this time loaded with baggage that holds everything that happened to it while on earth. It's not the same as the baggage the Aztecs or Egyptians carried—these aren't belongings to help make the afterlife more enjoyable. Rather, it is the sum of who a person was and what he or she did.

The Torah, the documentation for Jewish belief, dates back to the second millennium B.C.

"God's promised rewards as recorded in the Torah are consistently this-worldly and communal," according to Rabbi Elie Kaplan Spitz. The author of several books on Jewish beliefs, Spitz said in *Do Jews Believe in the Soul's Survival?* that although the Torah hardly addresses what happens after death, "There is a recurring phrase that affirms another realm of existence." Spitz said that the death of Abraham was recorded as, "he died, was gathered to his people, and was buried."

"Medieval and contemporary biblical scholars agree that 'gathered to his people' refers to soul, a quality of consciousness that persists and is rewarded with an eternal life on another plane," Spitz wrote.

CHRISTIAN BELIEF

Since the ancient Egyptians, there have been, more or less, organized religions, many of which were covered earlier in this chapter. But Christians believe that about 2,000 years ago, Jesus of Nazareth, the son of God, died and then was resurrected.

As Christian belief began to dominate European culture, the belief in heaven and hell that most Christians are familiar with, even if they don't totally adhere to it, began to shape afterlife belief (at least among those who were keeping notes).

Christians, to simplify things, were pretty sure your behavior on earth determined which place you would go—up or down. And those are the people who founded America.

Early American Beliefs

If you don't count the Native Americans—who were unaware of the fate that awaited them when Puritans first came to colonize America—the first white Americans were firm believers in the Christian view of heaven and hell.

> **EARLY WAKEUP CALL**
> The First Great Awakening, which took place from roughly 1730 to 1750 in America, helped shape the attitudes that led to the American Revolution, particularly the longing for a separation of church and state.

Among the Puritans who colonized the northeast of America were the Calvinists, who believed in predestination. There were a few elected to go to heaven, and everyone else, no matter how good they were, was going to hell. Predestination was adopted by many of the Protestant denominations that settled in New England—Congregationalists and Presbyterians, for the most part.

Many also believed the preaching of Jonathan Edwards. In 1741, his sermon in Enfield, Connecticut, "Sinners in the Hands of an Angry God," scared the living daylights out of his followers.

The sermon was part of the first Great Awakening religious movement, which, in the mid-1700s, began to reshape the way many of early America's Christians regarded religion, bringing a fire-and-brimstone flair that hadn't been there before.

Edwards told his audience, "There is nothing that keeps wicked men at any one moment out of hell, but the mere pleasure of God." But Edwards also posited that "the wicked" could save themselves by embracing Christ, which was a refreshing change from the Calvinist predestination theory that nothing you could do could keep you out of hell if you weren't one of the elect.

IT'S HOTTER DOWN SOUTH

According to the Pew survey, residents of Mississippi are the most likely in the United States to believe in hell, with 82 percent saying they believe in it. The least likely? The no-nonsense Yankees of New Hampshire and Vermont, where only 37 percent say they believe in hell.

By the nineteenth century, things were beginning to change in America. "In the medieval era, people believed that the purpose of the afterlife was to glorify God," said E. Brooks Holifield, a professor of comparative religion at Emory University in Atlanta. "But in the nineteenth century, the purpose was to be reunited with departed loved ones, and heaven, especially, was domesticated. It was an extension of relationships here."

Hell? Hell No!

Fast-forward to the 2008 Pew survey. While three-quarters of Americans believe in an afterlife—which some see as heaven and some see as something else—only 59 percent believe in hell. This is true even for the Reverend Damian Milliken, the Catholic priest and missionary in Tanzania, who was raised in a strict Catholic home and entered the seminary at age twelve. "I don't think there's any suffering after death," he said.

Alan F. Segal, a professor of religion at Barnard College and the author of *Life After Death: A History of the Afterlife in Western Religion* said that statistics showing that fewer Americans believe in hell are right on. "Hell is for nonbelievers, and most Americans don't believe there are nonbelievers next door, even if their religion is different," Segal told the *Boston Globe* after the Pew survey results were released. "They believe everyone has an equal chance at this life and the next."

RELIGION AND THE AFTERLIFE

It's not possible to discuss afterlife beliefs without also talking about religion. It's not necessary to be religious, or a member of a faith, to believe in an afterlife, but most of those who do believe are religious. And their afterlife beliefs are tied directly to what they believe about God.

The highest rate of belief in the Pew study was among Mormons. Some 98 percent of Mormons surveyed believed in an afterlife, with 88 percent saying they were "absolutely certain."

In the Pew survey, 81 percent of Protestants believed in an afterlife, with 62 percent classifying their belief as "absolutely certain." Only 12 percent said they didn't believe. These beliefs were strongest—86 percent—among Evangelical churches, but historically black churches came in at a strong 79 percent, and mainline Protestant churches had a 78 percent belief rate—all above the national average.

Among Catholics, 77 percent, still above the national average, believed in an afterlife, but only 45 percent were "absolutely certain."

Orthodox Christian religions had a 74 percent belief rate, with 47 percent absolutely certain.

In non-Christian religions, 39 percent of Jews believed in an afterlife, and only 16 percent were absolutely certain. Some 45 percent didn't believe in life after death.

Some 77 percent of Muslims believed in an afterlife, with 67 percent absolutely certain.

Buddhists had a 68 percent belief rate, with 32 percent being absolutely certain. Hindus were similar, with a 65 percent belief rate, and 33 percent absolutely certain.

Among those not affiliated with a religion, 48 percent believed in an afterlife.

Atheists had an 18 percent belief rate, but 75 percent didn't believe. Of the 18 percent that did, only 5 percent were absolutely certain.

Agnostics had a 35 percent belief rate and 45 percent nonbelief rate.

Secular humanists were split right down the middle—44 percent believed in an afterlife and 45 percent didn't.

Of those who were religious but unaffiliated with any religion, 66 percent believed in an afterlife and 22 percent didn't.

BELIEF HAS CHANGED

The Pew survey shows that Americans' belief in the afterlife is higher than it's been in decades. Some 74 percent of Americans interviewed for that survey believed in an afterlife, compared to 69 percent in 1973.

Some think it's even more than that. "I'm surprised it's not higher," said Paldrom Collins, of California, the former Buddhist nun.

Kendra Vaughn Hovey, a Massachusetts editor who holds a doctor of ministry degree from the University of Metaphysics and a PhD from the American Institute of Holistic Theology, echoed that thought: "I would have guessed that the statistics would be much higher."

E. Brooks Holifield, the Emory professor of comparative religions, also wasn't surprised by the high number. "I think that more people might believe in an afterlife because that is a focal theme in evangelical churches, and those churches have grown in recent years," Holifield said. (Evangelical belief involves a strict reading of the Bible, particularly the gospels; spreading the word; and the belief in being "born again" by accepting Jesus as savior). "Evangelicals are more likely to feel certain about an afterlife than a good number of mainline Protestants and liberal Catholics."

Andrew Gurevich, a philosophy and literature professor at Mount Hood Community College in Gresham, Oregon, has another take. "Millennialism, the global economic and climate crises, and the approaching enigma of 2012 seem to be increasing our collective apprehension about the future of our species," he said. "I just saw a news report that said that an area of the Midwest that normally gets about thirty-five tornadoes a year has experienced over 600 already, and they're just entering the period of peak activity. Two of the storms have been rated category 5, the highest ranking we give tornadoes. In this climate, it is not hard to imagine why people are increasingly starting to look elsewhere for hope in their future."

Debunking the Traditional

Both our survey and the Pew research shows that what's also changed are views on the traditional heaven-and-hell structure.

Anna Rossi, 75, a Maine bookseller who was brought up in a Catholic household, is a first-generation American. She said,

"We were taught the traditional heaven and hell. I believed it without question." She also believed the church's teaching that one must be a good churchgoer to go to heaven—that is, until her father died when she was a child. She said, "He was not a churchgoer, but was a good and generous person. I remember thinking at the time that there was no way he wasn't going to heaven. That may have been the beginning of my thinking that it is not all black and white." Now, at 75, she does not practice any religion. "But I still hope there is a greater power up there who listens to me."

Ken Shouler, author and philosophy professor, said only a small percentage of people abandon their own faiths.

"I had a statistic showing that only nine percent of Hindus leave their faith for another and the other faiths show a low number, too. Thus, I don't think their beliefs in the afterlife change much, since belief derives from the faith, which is stable."

Catherine Mills, 84, of Maine, a retired medical research assistant, is a practicing Catholic who believes in the traditional heaven and hell. "I was raised as a Roman Catholic and I believed that after death, you go directly to heaven if you're deserving of it or go to limbo to atone for sins before going to heaven. If you're in a state of mortal sin (extremely bad or evil), then you go to hell; I believed what I was taught."

These days, she said, "I still have those beliefs, but I think now more people go to heaven than I did then. I think a person who suffers in this life is already atoning for any sins and that limbo could well be here on earth before we die."

IT'S WHAT YOU MAKE IT

Americans' views of the afterlife in general, if they believe in it, have also changed over the years. Heaven is rarely an actual location where people land. "I'm a little worried about how crowded it would be," Father Damian Milliken, the Catholic priest said.

Almost all of those surveyed for this book who believe in an afterlife have a view of one that doesn't include heaven as an actual place. As you can imagine, this also shifts mightily from what they were taught, or believed, as children.

In the Billy Collins poem "The Afterlife," he writes that heaven is whatever you believe it to be and "Everyone is right as it turns out." Billy was raised by a mother who was a daily communicant, and a father who never left the house without his rosary beads and who said his nightly prayers kneeling by his bed. As a child, he said, "I believed in the standardized heaven, a place of clouds and harp music, which one entered through gates made entirely of pearl after receiving a blue card from a man after he had looked up your name in a big directory."

However, his views changed as he got older.

"I think I felt a shift away from this consoling picture when I realized that along with heaven came hell, especially as it was described in Joyce's *A Portrait of the Artist as a Young Man*. The famous sermon on hell is a parade of frightening images of an eternity filled with endless and relentless punishment.

"[In my own church] we were asked to imagine a mountain of sand a million miles high. That alone is enough to give you a sore neck. But then imagine further that once every million years a bird removes a single grain of sand. (I can't wait for the next one!) And after the entire mountain had been removed . . . well, my friends, that would not reduce your eternal sentence by one second! I left the chapel wondering what a bird would want with a grain of sand. An ant would have been a better choice."

Catholic teaching also made him reconsider, and he said he felt his belief in heaven falter: "I learned that St. Thomas listed as one of the delights of heaven the ability of the saved to behold the sufferings of the damned. I shuddered to think of the angels fighting for a front row seat. And you thought reading 'The Inferno' was a treat. Here's the real thing in real time, or rather no time."

Rhonda St. James, 49, a New Hampshire securities compliance manager who was also raised Catholic, is more succinct about why her beliefs have changed from the traditional ones she grew up with. "I can only theorize that it's the result of the slow accretion of experience, personal losses and internalizing nearly fifty years of information on this subject," she said. "Apparently my internal computer took in all the data and synthesized its own theorem."

Paldrom Collins (no relation to Billy), an author and counselor, was raised in several Christian traditions, starting with Southern Baptist, and was once a Buddhist nun. She still embraces her Buddhist beliefs and isn't surprised that people's views on the afterlife change as they mature.

"Life can have a big impact," she said. "The very nature of the ups and downs of this ride of life we are on can impact our view of the ride. Being present when someone dies can have a radical impact. Facing death, being diagnosed with a terminal illness, or surviving an incident in which death is faced head on can change feelings about this life and thus the afterlife."

She added that other people's beliefs, and what we read and see in the world around us, also have an impact on us. We filter that through our own experience, and our views change.

Very few of those interviewed had a clear concept of what the afterlife might be.

Ian Clark, 37, a New Hampshire sportswriter and author of science fiction/fantasy novels, said, "I'm not sure I believe in heaven and hell. If anything, I believe that there might be some form of heaven, but not hell. Perhaps if there is some 'reward' it's that there is an afterlife and you are able to meet up with old friends and family, and the penalty of hell would be that there is nothing, your ride is over." He added, "I don't think the idea of a utopian heaven is real, but more that the afterlife is a lingering presence of your soul and consciousness that is able to observe the goings-on of the living in some way (as a ghost, I suppose)."

Ashleen O'Gaea, a writer and Wiccan priestess, said, "I find [the afterlife] incomprehensible, but not in an intimidating or engulfing way. I trust in the process of life–death–rebirth because I see it taking place all around me, all the time." And she added, "I expect it to be awesome and wonderful and that it will be one of those, 'Oh! Well, of course!' experiences."

This Is It

Those interviewed who don't believe in an afterlife are equally sure of their beliefs.

"I believe that people die and that's it—they're dead," says Elizabeth Daniels, the executive secretary/office manager. "I do not think that a soul or a spirit goes to heaven or hell to either have tea and crumpets with whoever or whatever God is, or to be eternally tortured by a red devil creature with horns and a pitchfork. . . . I think people just die—the same way a rose withers or weeds get pulled from the dirt or a cow gets put down for ground beef. No one ever considers the spirit or soul of a living being that they didn't love or care about. Those things just die— they cease to exist."

Martin Scattergood, 53, an engineer who owns his own company and lives in Germany, doesn't believe in a god, but he upholds spiritual values despite the fact that he doesn't worship. When it comes to the afterlife, he said, "My vision is that it is the end. There is nothing. I believe my bodily presence ceases to absolutely exist."

He comes to this belief honestly. In 2005, he contracted an illness, stopped breathing and was seconds away from death. After waking from a coma, he was on life support, completely paralyzed, in severe pain and unable to communicate. He said that on two occasions, he wanted to die. "I wanted to escape from my new horrible world. As far as I was concerned at that time, death was also total finality."

John Reed, a Massachusetts high school teacher, said his afterlife belief is not spiritual. "I believe people live in others' memories. So long as we continue to have an effect through memory, we have an 'afterlife.' So when I teach a class using a hint my mentor gave me, he is still there. When I keep lists the way my grandfather did, he's with me. But what about the person who taught [those who came before] those habits? Unless someone else remembers them, they're gone."

Mark Henderson, 53, a counselor, was raised as a Methodist. He now describes himself as a former pastor turned atheist. As someone who has dealt with death and dying for most of his life, as a funeral director's son, a pastor who gave his first sermon at the age of 19, a hospital chaplain, and now a counselor, he said he holds "no belief in an afterlife whatsoever."

A few years ago he beat cancer. A year ago it came back. When he took the Afterlife Survey, he had just been told that nothing more could be done for him. He said that as he faces death, he is not consumed with thoughts of what will happen next.

"I've got to say that the older I've gotten, the more reason I've found not to be so bored with this life that the prospect of a next holds much appeal. There is so much richness and beauty present in this life that it's almost seemed unappreciative to hope for 'something better' in a next life."

CHAPTER TWO

A MINISTER, A RABBI, AND A PRIEST WALK INTO HEAVEN

Much of modern-day afterlife belief is defined by Judeo-Christian tradition—the culture in which most of us were raised in and what much of American society considers the norm. Many of our survey responders come from this tradition, and their views have been shaped by it.

Family belief and religious upbringing shape people's early views about the afterlife. For Christians, it's always been pretty simple, no matter what the denomination. Jesus ascended into heaven so that humans on earth could be forgiven of their sins.

And, depending on the denomination and whether the person is Catholic or Protestant, the road to heaven is smoother the better person you are or the more you adhere to your denomination's rules for salvation.

Many Christian denominations also believe in limbo or purgatory. The belief in what those are varies according to denomination, but most simply believe they are a way station for those not quite ready for heaven yet or for those who can't make it to heaven but aren't bad enough for hell.

Some Christian denominations also believe it's all going to come together in a giant apocalypse that was written about in the book of Revelation, the last section of the New Testament. The book of Revelation, written by "John" (although whether it's the apostle John or someone else is open to interpretation) says that

Jesus, heaven, and hell will all come together in a battle of good and evil, and the evil will be vanquished and the good saved.

Some Christian denominations are founded on this part of the Bible. Others, such as Catholicism, are more focused on other aspects of achieving salvation.

And then there's hell . . . .

For centuries, it was bigger than heaven in many Christians minds. A place of suffering and punishment so bad that fear of it should be enough to keep you on the straight and narrow.

IT'S THE END OF THE WORLD . . .

Occasionally, a Christian extremist who believes in the rapture—that moment when God descends from heaven, claims those who have been good enough, and leaves the rest to perish in a violent apocalypse—will set a date for it, most recently May 21, 2011. Harold Camping, 89, a retired civil engineer and founder of Family Radio Worldwide, believed that his numerological calculations based on the Bible set that as the date that "the faithful" would be brought into heaven by God, while the rest of the world would stay on earth for some harsh punishment. You're reading this, so it's clear his numbers were off. It wouldn't be the first time. Earlier he predicted it would happen in 1994. When it didn't, he said it wasn't that he was wrong, but rather that date was the end of "the church age," the time when people in Christian churches could be saved. The more recent date was the date when only those outside of what his followers call "irredeemably corrupt" churches would be the ones brought into heaven.

But, as the Pew survey shows, many people—nearly half—no longer believe in hell.

Jewish belief is a little more complicated. According to the Pew survey, only 39 percent of Jews believe in an afterlife. And of them, only 16 percent are "absolutely certain."

"As with most questions in Judaism, there are two answers," said Rabbi Ilene Schneider. "One: 'It depends (on whom you ask)' and two: 'Who knows?'

"I'm not trying to be flippant, but the views do vary, depending on how traditional the respondent is. The ideas of an afterlife and resurrection are central to many Orthodox beliefs, but actually stem from Jews' taking on superstitions and beliefs from the people they lived among. And Judaism evolves and changes; many modern Jews who are not Orthodox in philosophy or theology (even if they are in practice) 'transvalue' traditional beliefs, interpreting them in metaphorical, nontheistic terms."

In our survey, some of those interviewed were staunch in their religion's afterlife beliefs. But many, whether Christian or Jewish, met in the middle—that great area of "I think there's something there. I hope there's something there. But I just don't know."

MODERN-DAY CHRISTIAN BELIEVERS

Modern Christians have expanded their views on what an afterlife may mean. Most believe in, or hope for, something after death. Most think that if they are good people, that afterlife will hold good things for them. But the specifics of their belief are as different as people themselves.

Heaven . . . or Something Like It

"Many Christians now tend to interpret the Bible figuratively," according to E. Brooks Holifield, the Emory University professor of comparative religion. "They see both heaven and hell as metaphors that point to mysteries that are not fully within the range of our comprehension. Many still believe in an afterlife, but they tend to believe in the Greek concept of the immortality of the soul rather than the New Testament conception of the resurrection of the body.

"Actually, the New Testament doesn't say much about heaven; it talks of the Kingdom of God, or the Kingdom of Heaven. People tend to fit their religion to their own presuppositions."

In the Pew survey, Christians were the biggest believers in an afterlife, in numbers that ranged from 74 percent to 98 percent, depending on the denomination. And our survey showed similar numbers. But our responders also agreed with Holifield—most of them fit their perception of the afterlife into their own mold. Christians today, even those who consider themselves strict followers of their religion, still qualify their belief in heaven and hell—even the ones who say they believe in it.

"I was raised in a traditional family with strong religious roots," said Brian McHugh, the 35-year-old New Hampshire funeral director. "Parochial elementary schooling followed by Catholic high school and a Jesuit college education. I never really questioned what I was being taught, as it all seemed to make sense. When you are young and most impressionable, teachers, parents, and clergy working in combination spreading the same message didn't allow for much creativity when it came to matters of the afterlife." Now, as an adult who sees death every day, he said he firmly believes what he was taught at an early age.

But even with that firm belief, he sees room for variation, depending on the person. "As a funeral director, I routinely see people facing the most difficult times in their lives, questioning what this whole game of life is all about. The more I see people struggle to understand why their loved one has left this life, the more I appreciate and comprehend why humans should believe in an afterlife, be it the traditional heaven and hell or some other variation more suitable to their own beliefs."

Matt McSorley, 42, the newspaper editor who just completed a master's degree in counseling and also is a devout Catholic, is as strong, if not stronger, in his beliefs than ever. "My own reading of Augustine and Aquinas is more compelling to me than any scholarship that posits the nonexistence of God." As a Catholic, the existence of God is directly tied to the existence of an afterlife. "Until you posed the question, it never occurred to me that they could be separated," he said.

But he added that he believes those who have different beliefs than he will also be part of the afterlife. Even those Christians who have strayed from their religion or have drifted into agnosticism still hold on to those beliefs in which they were raised, in some form or another.

"As a child, I held to the traditional belief of going to heaven upon death, despite not being raised in a religious environment," said Scott Moulton, 47, a New Hampshire investment services manager who was raised in a loosely Christian home.

Now, as an adult, he tries to honor those tenets, "But I am more skeptical about the traditional concepts . . . . My beliefs have changed with respect to what I believe the afterlife 'is' and the 'form' it may take."

Elizabeth Daniels, the 26-year-old executive assistant/office manager who was raised in a Pentecostal family on one side and Southern Baptist on the other, said her views have definitely changed. "My mind is not in the same place as it was when I was a child. When I was a child, I didn't understand anything. They told me to believe in God to save my soul, and I said 'okay.' But in my child mind, God was a literal man sitting on a cloud that floated around in circles just outside of the planet earth. He was amazing and mighty and had the power to reward and punish every human deed."

She said hell was a "red fiery place," and, "God controlled the gates to one location and the devil dragged bad people down to the other location against their will and treated them badly.

"Now, as an adult, I believe that it might be possible for a human being to retain his or her sentience after death, while they lose their humanity." But she added that while she believes "when you're dead, you're dead," she really just doesn't know. "I am but a lowly human being—not meant to know, no matter what I think I believe."

Purgatory, Limbo, and Hell

Even the Reverend Damian Milliken, the Catholic priest, doesn't believe the black-and-white heaven, hell, and purgatory scenario. He says he believes purgatory and limbo are the creation of philosophers. He said he doesn't like the idea that a person can "earn or buy" his or her way into heaven—and he doesn't believe in hell at all.

"I don't think there's any suffering after death," he said. "Even for Al Capone or someone like that." He said that he believes God is forgiving and compassionate, and, "No one is so bad that they are going to be condemned to suffer eternally."

Even Hitler?

"Even Hitler," he said firmly and with conviction, adding the line from the Apostles' Creed, a prayer recited at every Catholic Mass. "We believe," he said, in "the forgiveness of sins, and life everlasting."

Anna Rossi, 75, the bookseller, who was raised in a strict immigrant Catholic home but now does not practice any religion, said, "I still find myself praying to former relatives, God, and some saints."

John Reed, the high school teacher, who was raised Catholic, said as a child he believed "all the people I love are in heaven looking down on me, and if I misbehave, I'll burn in hell. I also grew up believing in limbo and purgatory. I said many prayers to release people from purgatory."

ABANDON ALL HOPE . . .

While belief in an actual hell has waned over the centuries, it had a pretty good run for the first couple thousand years of Christianity. And people still frequently refer to one of the most vivid, scary, and enduring visions of hell, Dante's *Inferno*. *Inferno* (which is Italian for hell), is actually just one part of Dante Alighieri's fourteenth-century epic poem *The Divine Comedy*. Dante's hell had nine circles, each more grisly than the one before. And the sign at the entrance? "Abandon all hope, ye who enter here." Not to be outdone, a few centuries later, John Milton wrote his epic poem *Paradise Lost*, which at great length chronicles the Christian view of the fall of man, with Satan getting a starring role. These musings on hell are considered two of the most influential and enduring works of literature.

But now he doesn't believe in an afterlife, except for the legacy a person leaves behind. That said, he also said he thought some of the rituals of the church that were designed to help him get to heaven after he died still have merit. "As a young Catholic, I went to confession, but never knew what it was about," he said. "I thought the priest was looking into my soul, performing an operation. I thought the penance was just a formality. How many Hail Marys I sped through! But as I grew older, and dropped away from it, I realized that confession is a valid psychological tool: it focuses you and tells you what you know to be true, even if you don't want to admit it."

And April McLeod, 45, a New Hampshire dog sitter, said she was raised in a fundamentalist Christian home, where heaven and hell were constant enticements and threats. She said that the judgment from both her parents and the church "made me believe maybe I was going to hell when I died."

April continued, "[It] nearly convinced me that God had the same feelings of judgment toward me, and as a result of those beliefs I was certain I was going to hell when I died. Once I stopped going to church I began the healing process and during that time I was reminded of what God is really like: a God who forgives and a God who wants everyone to live with him in the afterlife."

You will read more about John's and April's change of heart about the religions in which they were raised.

MODERN JEWISH BELIEF

The Jewish faith has always had a looser view of the afterlife than Christianity.

Each person is endowed with a *neshamah*, or soul, that links him or her to the divine, according to Rabbi Elie Kaplan Spitz. "Upon our death, our neshamah returns to its source with memories gathered and a record of deeds," he wrote in *Do Jews Believe in the Soul's Survival?* "It is our life's task, the Ba'al Shem Tov (the founder of Hasidism, 1700–1760) taught, to cultivate and elevate our neshamah through acts of connection to God, particularly acts of compassion. Judaism, in contrast to many other religions, places its emphasis on this life. God's promised rewards as recorded in the Torah are consistently this-wordly and communal."

Lots of Wiggle Room

Rabbi Ilene Schneider said that the ancient faith has evolved over the centuries and continues to evolve regarding afterlife beliefs.

"The idea of an afterlife and resurrection are central to many Orthodox beliefs, but actually stem from Jews' taking on superstitions and beliefs from the people they lived among. And Judaism evolves and changes; many modern Jews who are not Orthodox in philosophy or theology (even if they are in practice) 'transvalue' traditional beliefs, interpreting them in metaphorical, nontheistic terms."

She said one thing has always remained true about the religion and is still a major tenet today. "Judaism has always put the emphasis on this world, as it's the only one we know," she said. "We must behave well here because it's the right thing to do, not because we are looking forward to a reward after we die."

But the thought of an afterlife persists: "We know that justice is often not meted out in this world, that the wicked are not always punished, and that good people suffer. So we need to cling to the hope that the evil-doers will eventually get what they deserve."

Andrew Gurevich, the philosophy and literature professor, said Jewish belief, which has been flexible since it began, got a huge jolt last century. "Jews firmly believed that they would be blessed by God in *this* life for their obedience to the Covenant. The afterlife was really not part of the deal originally. When the Jews suffered in this life, it could be explained as either arising from their own sinfulness and disobedience, or as spiritual character building; helping the faithful to grow in the virtues of patience, forgiveness, hospitality, and compassion," he said.

"The Holocaust changed all of that. No theological argument could be made from within most rabbinical circles to satisfy the people's emotional, visceral need to know why God had abandoned them to this darkest of all evils. Jews in Auschwitz actually put Yahweh on trial. They had a judge and jury, defense and prosecution, and even called witnesses. The jury deliberated and found him guilty of crimes against humanity. I am not making this up.

"At that moment, a significant portion of Judaism lost its messianic and metaphysical foundation (at least symbolically) and became a sort of Semitic (which means, in this case, relating strictly to Jewish belief) version of Buddhism: a system of practical wisdom rooted in observation and intended to help one navigate the 'real' world, not necessarily prepare for the next one."

He added, "Obviously a large part of the Jewish community rejected this whole thing as silliness or blasphemy. Most Orthodox Jews still await the Messiah in either a spiritual or political context."

Barbara Grandberg, 60, a retired Massachusetts teacher, was raised in a Jewish home. "I was told Jews do not believe in an afterlife, and I never questioned it," she said. She considers herself a nonpracticing Jew, but as far as an afterlife goes, "I'm not sure. When putting my cats [down], I tell them to say hi to their brothers."

Kendra Vaughn Hovey, a metaphysician, was also raised in a Jewish home. "Even as a Jewish child, I knew nothing of hell, and now I do not believe in it either."

She added, "I personally believe God is energy or spirit. As such, we live by the laws of natural order that govern the universe and never change. Knowing God as energy, there is no doubt in my mind that when I die, my spirit will unite with the spirit of God and I will be at peace and at rest."

Caren Gittleman, 55, a Michigan writer, was also raised in a Jewish home. "I was born Jewish, but we had virtually no discussion of religion in our home. As a child, I was extremely fearful of death and the thought of dying. I would lie in bed thinking about it and then count out how many years I had till it happened. I thought that I had to go through all of life's rituals first—graduating high school, going to college, marrying, having kids, etc. It used to comfort me to think that. It never dawned on me that one could die without completing any of the above."

She said dying still scares her, but she definitely believes in an afterlife.

"I probably believed in a combination. Part of me believes there is definitely a heaven and hell, but when I think about heaven I wonder why they don't run out of room up there?" But Caryn, who blogs about cats, added, "Another part of me thinks that you come back as an animal. In my case, I always thought I would come back as a dolphin or . . . a cat (of course)."

TWO FAITHS MERGE

Many of our respondents—whether brought up in a Christian faith, or Jewish, whether strict followers of the religion, casual observers, or agnostic—were clear: it's really hard to be certain of what awaits us after death.

But they were equally clear that what you do on this earth is what is important.

"I've boiled it down to a couple reliable rules," says Rhonda St. James, the securities compliance manager and former Catholic. "Whatever seems to be the most difficult thing to do in any given situation, is probably the right thing to do; the Golden Rule is not a good choice if you routinely treat yourself like crap, and life is too short to waste your time with jerks. Probably a gross simplification and not too many people would line up to join my church."

And in her "church" there is an afterlife, "in one form or another, just not in the way that any of us have envisioned." She added that she isn't really sure what her own vision of it is.

"I believe that we should lead a good life no matter what," said Anna Rossi. "Many people who believe in an afterlife are the cause of much suffering in this world."

Barbara Grandberg, the former teacher, said it succinctly. "It's what we do now that gives our life meaning."

The Reverend Damian Milliken, the Catholic priest, said that the actual concept of heaven is much more complicated than most people's vision of it. "We're not all going to be on the same deck of a cruise ship, or something like that," he said. But he added that in his long experience, people do agree on one thing: "I think that people feel that how they live their lives will be some determining factor in what happens after death."

CHAPTER THREE
DÉJÀ VU ALL OVER AGAIN

Eastern beliefs—particularly reincarnation—used to be considered way too far out there for traditionalists to consider part of their own afterlife beliefs. But the concept of a soul living many lives has become more mainstream. It's also a concept that Tibetan Buddhism, Hinduism, Zen, and other Eastern religions have embraced for thousands of years. While it's more complicated than whether you come back as a dolphin or dung beetle, reincarnation is something that gives many of our survey respondents food for thought.

While the majority of Americans wouldn't say they practice one of the Eastern religions—Hinduism, Buddhism, Jainism, Zen, or any of their offshoots—many of our respondents felt a kinship with tenets of these religions.

And that's not surprising, because although many of us were raised on heaven and hell, many who responded—like many people in the modern world—are getting away from those beliefs. And the Eastern religions speak of a continuing universal energy that appeals to many of our respondents, even if they can't define what exactly it is in terms of their religious or spiritual beliefs.

The basis of these Eastern religions is the idea of reincarnation—not only as something that occurs after the body dies, but as a huge influence on a how a person lives his or her life.

And that's something many of our respondents embrace wholeheartedly—or at least think is a neat idea.

WHAT ARE THE EASTERN RELIGIONS?

Hinduism is the basis for the other well-known Eastern religions, Buddhism and Jainism. These three religions are some of the most ancient religions in the world that are still practiced today. They all embrace karma and reincarnation. Karma, that notion that's worked its way into daily modern conversation, is the belief that your actions affect your future lives.

Hinduism

According to philosophy professor Ken Shouler, more than any other major religion, Hinduism celebrates the breadth and depth of its complex, multileveled spectrum of beliefs. "Hinduism encompasses all forms of belief and worship. It has been said that no religious idea in India ever dies; it merely combines with the new ideas that arise in response to it."

He said the philosophy includes the principles that real nature is divine, that the aim of humans is to realize this, and that all religions are essentially in agreement. Hinduism doesn't have one god, but it "offers a plethora of ideas—a metaphor for the gods," Shouler said. "It has been called a civilization and congregation of religions. Hinduism has no beginning, no founder, no central authority, no hierarchy, and no organization. Every attempt to classify or define Hinduism has proved to be unsatisfactory in one way or another."

He added that, "Hindus see their religion as a continuous, seemingly eternal, existence—not just a religion but a way of life. Its collection of customs, moral obligations—known as dharma— traditions, and ideals far exceed the recent Christian and Western secularist tendency to think of religion primarily as a system of beliefs. Hinduism has come to cover an incredibly wide range of concepts and concerns, including karma, methods for attaining salvation, and spiritual release from earthly existence."

Hindus believe in karma. And karma plays a huge role in reincarnation.

"In more technical terms, Hindus accept the doctrine of transmigration and rebirth, and believe that previous acts are the factors that determine the condition into which a being is reborn in one form or another," Shouler wrote. "The idea of reincarnation is virtually universal in India."

Hindus are usually cremated when they die, because to be reincarnated, all you need is a soul, not a body.

Buddhism

Buddhism centers around one's purpose in life—dharma—and the Four Noble Truths. Shouler said, "Buddha taught that the supreme good of life is nirvana, 'the extinction' or 'blowing out' of suffering and desire and awakening to what is most real."

Buddha means "enlightened," and Buddhism also teaches pacifism and nonviolence; hence the lack of belief in punishment of sins.

Jainism

Jainism is a little less known in the United States—possibly because its philosophy of shedding all material things as a way to stay away from bad karma probably doesn't appeal to the American idea of consumerism and material gain. Its name comes from the Sanskrit word for "to conquer," and the point of that means conquering one's ego and feelings of selfishness, hate, and greed. Jainism has been around since the sixth century B.C. and sprung directly from Hinduism. It stresses reverence for life, celibacy, and moral conduct.

Zen

Zen is another school of Buddhism that embraces the idea that enlightenment is attained through the wisdom of experience.

Remember the scene in *Caddyshack* when Chevy Chase tells the young golfer, "Be the ball"? That's the essence of Zen.

JAINISM: A GENTLE BELIEF

Mahatma Gandhi was influenced by the Jain principle of ahimsa, which is commonly thought of as simply nonviolence but is actually more complex. It's not only the principle of not harming others, but also being kind to nature itself. Mahavira, who is believed to have created the tenets of Jainism, is quoted as saying, "You are that which you wish to harm." The website *http://arcworld.org* says, "This is the positive aspect of nonviolence: to practice an attitude of compassion towards all life. Jains pray that forgiveness and friendliness may reign throughout the world and that all living beings may cherish each other. This ancient Jain principle teaches that all of nature is bound together, and says that if one does not care for nature one does not care for oneself." It is easy to see how this philosophy and reincarnation are tied into one another.

THE GROWING POPULARITY OF REINCARNATION

Reincarnation is one of the oldest afterlife beliefs in existence, stemming from those ancient Eastern religions covered in this chapter. The belief that a person's soul will return in a different body "seems to offer one of the most attractive explanations of humanity's origin and destiny," wrote Ernest Valea, on *www.comparativereligion.com*.

It is the foundation of many Eastern religions, but it hasn't gotten a lot of play in the heavily Christian United States. In fact, some Christian religions, particularly Catholicism, fervently reject the idea of a soul's reincarnation, saying it's in direct conflict with the church's teaching that the soul lives eternally.

While many philosophers and writers, particularly Carl Jung and American philosopher William James, gave reincarnation some credence, the general public was not as open minded. Those who grew up in the sixties and seventies may be familiar with the ribbing that actress Shirley MacLaine has taken in the media for her very vocal reincarnation beliefs.

IT'S PRONOUNCED "YOUNG"

Who's this Carl Jung that people keep throwing out there when they talk about afterlife beliefs? You may be wondering. It's okay if you're not familiar with him—to English speakers, his name is pronounced "young" (more or less). He was a Swiss psychiatrist who founded analytical psychiatry. More importantly, for our purposes, he theorized the "collective unconscious": all living things share an unconscious mind, with the same experiences and existence. Think about it for a little while. It will blow your mind.

But more recently, as Americans have expanded their beliefs on religion and the afterlife, belief in reincarnation has picked up steam among people with mainstream beliefs who aren't necessarily followers of Hinduism, Buddhism, or Jainism, and there is more acceptance of reincarnation as a possibility.

The Pew survey shows 24 percent of those polled believe in reincarnation. This tallies with a 2009 Harris poll that put the number at 20 percent.

"It is accepted not only by adherents of Eastern religions and New Age spirituality, but also by many who don't share such esoteric interests and convictions. To know that you lived many lives before this one and that there are many more to come is a very attractive perspective from which to judge the meaning of life," Ernest Valea wrote on *www.comparativereligion.com*.

Our survey participants, for the most part, agree. Some are true believers, some are hopeful, and some take a whimsical view that it sure would be nice.

HISTORY OF REINCARNATION BELIEF

While there are signs that Druids, Ancient Greeks, and others dating back to the Iron Age—about 1200 B.C.—had reincarnation beliefs, it really came into its own with the Eastern religions. As we learned earlier, Hindu beliefs were the first to fully embrace reincarnation as a basis for a religion. It was also adopted in Chinese Taoism a few centuries later with the spread of Buddhism. As belief in reincarnation spread, its exact meaning morphed, according to the culture and religion of the society.

Most people simplify reincarnation. They believe it simply means you come back as a dolphin, cocker spaniel, or cockroach. In fact, it's very complicated, and it's tied in with both people's karma—their behavior—and people's dharma—their purpose in life. In Hinduism, *moksha,* or the process of the soul's release from the cycle of reincarnation, is the ultimate spiritual goal.

If a person has bad karma, they don't reach *moksha*. Once they do reach *moksha*, they reunite with Brahman and end the cycle of suffering. Ken Shouler said, "Those who do not accept that their being is identical with Brahman are thought to be deluded—in such cases, you might say that the atman is clouded by *maya*, illusion. The only possible solution is to come to the realization that the core of human personality (atman) really is Brahman. The attachment to worldly goods blocks this understanding because it is an obsession that prevents people from reaching salvation and eternal peace.

"To add to the difficulties in understanding this process, meanings and interpretations differ from one Hindu school to another. In spite of that, most of them agree that moksha is the highest purpose in life," said Shouler.

> ## PLATONIC MYSTERY
>
> While the ancient Greek philosopher Plato is often said to have supported belief in reincarnation, scholars differ on that fact as much as they differ on, well, reincarnation itself. While he referred to reincarnation several times in his writings, many scholars believe the references were allegories and not meant to be taken literally. As we remember from school, Plato's teachings were designed to make us consider questions and get our brains working. He rarely gave us the answers.

Europeans later changed the meaning of reincarnation, and it has evolved among those who believe in it but don't practice Eastern religions. But New Age belief sees it as more progressing toward eternal knowledge, rather than trying to escape the pain of the person one was in the past. What we have in the twenty-first century, most religious scholars agree, is something less complicated than the Eastern concept—something that allows the actual person to somehow keep returning.

In modern belief, many feel reincarnation simply is the belief that if you're good, you come back as something really great—a dolphin seems to be the popular choice—and if you're bad, you come back as something miserable and ugly. "Reincarnation seems like an amusing abstraction," said our survey responder Rhonda St. James. "Everybody wants to come back as a dolphin (without the tuna net), but no one considers that they might return as a dung beetle."

THE TRUE BELIEVERS

Former Buddhist nun Paldrom Collins explained that belief in reincarnation, and the afterlife itself, is not something that's easy to spell out. It's certainly more difficult than the dolphin– dung beetle scenario, especially because there is no simple yes or no answer as to whether, or how, it exists. "It involves looking at the nature of reality itself, our perception of what is real, or perception that we 'exist.' And this is difficult to speak about because we are bound by the perception of our senses, our brains, our words, the reality as we are able to experience it through our senses and describe it with words bound inside the reality."

Paldrom pointed out that the very word afterlife is based on our concept of time (after) and our concept of life "which inher- ently assumes existence, that is, 'I am alive, I have a life, I exist.'"

She said if those two assumptions—that time is linear and that we exist—are true, then the focus on "what happens after I die?" shields us from asking the questions about time and existence itself that might reveal more true answers to our queries about the afterlife.

"Imagine for a moment that everything, everyone, every thought, every piece of light, feeling, emotion—all is one. The electricity that is powering the light on the table and dryer in the basement is the same electricity. In the lamp it appears as light; in the dryer it appears as heat. In the same way, the source that is expressing itself as you and as me is the same source."

She cited the common example of one droplet of water in the ocean—the belief that while we think we are all unique, we are all the same drops in the ocean that make one big whole. "The drop may perceive itself as an individual drop, but even without aware- ness, it is still part of the ocean, always has been, always will be."

She explained that this concept is "the heart, the essence, the pinnacle of Buddhist teaching."

So, back to reincarnation. "If the apparent birth of our individual life stream is simply that of a drop in the ocean that has lost track of the fact that it is a part of the ocean, then our apparent death can be viewed as simply merging back into oceanic awareness.

"In this way, those who believe we simply 'disappear' at death are correct in a way. As are those who believe we 'go to heaven (or hell).' It's all a matter of the view through a particular filter.

"With this sort of analogy, the mind can maybe start to have a referent for the Buddhist teaching of no one dies, no one is born. The whole investigation of an afterlife gets turned inside out."

As with many ancient beliefs, those who are not of an Eastern religion but who also practice the beliefs that go back way before religion was even a concept also feel strongly about reincarnation.

John Bear Mitchell, of the Penobscot tribe, said, "I don't believe in reincarnation as (changing) back to a human, but I do believe we are given the opportunity to come back to Earth as an earthly animal to provide for our people."

Ken Shouler said while all indigenous beliefs can't be lumped under one belief heading, the idea of reincarnation among ancient people of all walks of life was common and still holds sway in their culture today (more about this in Chapter 4). "Death is considered a transition, and many outcomes are possible following death," he said.

And for many, that is reincarnation.

Shirley MacLaine: Reincarnation Poster Girl

Probably no celebrity is more famous, or infamous, for belief in reincarnation than actor Shirley MacLaine. In fact, most people probably know this fact about her more readily than they can name the movie for which she won an Oscar (1983's *Terms of Endearment*). This doesn't seem to bother MacLaine. She has devoted an entire page of her website, *www.shirleymaclaine.com*, to her beliefs.

"We may not consciously bring old knowledge with us into new lives," she writes on her website, "but sometimes it seems to seep through into our present experience. In this physical form, I have searched for my truth in this arena. I have discovered knowledge of other physical lives, relationships that felt as if they had been in place forever and foreign soils that felt like home."

Among her experiences, MacLaine tells of encountering herself in a former life while walking across Spain on the Santiago de Compostela Camino pilgrimage. "I discovered a part of me that led to a greater understanding of myself. I also realized the karmic importance of some of the people that have been close to me in this existence." She says that the realizations she has experienced in her life "have helped, inspired and added to my whole being. They have assisted in my better understanding myself and those around me."

WOULDN'T IT BE NICE . . .

Most of the respondents to our survey have a more amorphous, uncertain view of reincarnation. It sounds nice, and maybe it even exists, but they're not sure. Those who wonder about it span the range of beliefs from those who ask, "Why not?" to those who think, "I wish."

"I think it's a possibility," said Anna Rossi, the 75-year-old bookseller. "Our bodies are just recyclable matter, so why can't a soul enter any body? If there are souls . . . ."

Barbara Grandberg, the retired teacher, has a view tied to reality and forged from her years in classrooms. "I'm not sure," she said. "It's sort of scary that you can come back in a way you don't want to. I worked with students with severe special needs. I've had students who had no concept that they even existed. No quality of life. I would not want to come back that way."

Scott Moulton, the investment services manager, has a view that meshes nicely with Paldrom Collins's Buddhist take, that we are part of a greater one, so reincarnation is not necessarily a bodily experience, but more one of energy. "I don't believe that I would come back as another version of myself at some time in the future or even as a human being. I believe that there is potentially some pool of life force or energy that might be recycled into some other form of life or consciousness," he said. "Life force is energy—science tells us that energy can neither be created nor destroyed—but it can be converted into other uses, which is what I believe will happen upon death."

Those who practice more alternative religions have a looser take on reincarnation and other similar beliefs. Ashleen O'Gaea, the Wiccan priestess, said, "I'm curious. I wonder two things about any set of beliefs and interpretations: first, how it feels to the believer, and second, what kind of behavior it generates. As a Wiccan, I understand that with few exceptions, we can change not only our behaviors, but our feelings; of course, not everyone knows or accepts that—so if a 'belief' is imposed on someone, I have a different opinion than when a person has embraced it willingly."

Arin Murphy-Hiscock, another Wiccan, echoed O'Gaea's view. "I, like most others in pagan paths, fully embrace [alternative beliefs like reincarnation] as part of how people express their feelings and perceptions of the life cycle. Every perception and interpretation is valid within the context of any given individual's personal system of beliefs."

Kendra Vaughn Hovey, a metaphysician, said, "I prefer not to focus or concern myself with such things. When an incident happens and I think it could be a 'spirit among us,' I smile and perhaps spend a moment in wonder or reflection of a loved one passed, but I prefer to spend my energy on the wonder and mystery of God." However, explained Kendra, beliefs such as reincarnation "are not alternate beliefs to a New Ager or pagan and many find tremendous amounts of comfort in exploring them more deeply."

NO WAY, NO HOW

Those in our survey who don't believe in reincarnation stand firm about it, but understand its appeal.

Ian Clark, the sports writer and science fiction/fantasy author, said, "Reincarnation is a tough one for me. I don't really believe in it, yet things like children who can speak languages they should not know and other strange documented cases are interesting."

"I do not believe in reincarnation, but I don't consider it baloney, either," said Elizabeth Daniels. "My mother passed away when I was young and I always wondered what happened to her after her heart stopped beating." She said she thinks humans believe in an afterlife because they don't want to accept the death of a loved one. "They want to hang onto at least one little thing. I toyed with the idea of reincarnation once, when I would wake up on some mornings and my oldest dog would be sitting right in front of my face next to my pillow, staring at me. I thought that maybe my mother's soul was somehow within the dog, and my mother hadn't left me alone on earth with an abusive father and no other parental love to fall back on, even if only a warm thought or feeling. And to me, in that way of thinking, the look on my dog's face couldn't just be a dog looking at me. I thought I saw a human sense of intellect and understanding in her eyes. But the human mind can create whatever it wants the world to be.

"I now think my dog is just very special—extremely special, actually—but I do not think she is my mother."

Ilene Schneider, the rabbi, also doesn't believe.

"But I do not challenge anyone's right to believe what they want," she added. She said when a relative was killed in a car accident, her grandmother told her during the shiva that she'd had a dream about the boy's mother, who had died shortly before. The dead woman had come to her in a dream and confessed she was lonely.

"My grandmother was American born, fairly secular, but I was not going to tell her that her dream was just an extension of her own mind, reflecting her attempts to understand a tragedy. It gave her comfort to think my cousin and his grandmother were [connecting] again."

As it turns out, those firmest in their religious beliefs and those who eschew religious beliefs altogether firmly deny the idea of reincarnation.

"I do not believe in reincarnation," said Brian McHugh, the Catholic funeral director. "I believe we are given one chance on this earth to use our gifts to better the world around us. For me, reincarnation leaves too many variables unanswered. For example, how many chances do we have to get it right? What happens if I come back to this earth as a dung beetle? Now how can I make the world a better place for all living things? It is too confusing and quite scary to ponder."

Jim Robidoux, 52, a New Hampshire sheet-metal worker, doesn't see reincarnation fitting in with what he's learned from the Bible. "Reincarnation as I have heard, is most likely wrong," he said. "I don't know all the ins and outs of God himself, but I do believe scripture is right. We now see through a fog and at the end of time we will see clearly like God does. We are not God and can only handle so much. If God were using reincarnation, everything we read in the Bible would be skewed."

And Martin Scattergood, the business owner and engineer, looks at it from a completely pragmatic point of view. "Our bodies and presence on this earth cease to exist in any physical or nonphysical way after death," he said. "I do not believe our nonphysical body or spirit or soul can exist in any form after death. Therefore, reincarnation is not possible."

But, in agreement with most of our responders, both those who believe in reincarnation and those who don't, he added, "Our memories live on in those people we have known."

CHAPTER FOUR

SPIRITS AND SHADOWS

Some of the world's most enduring afterlife beliefs were formed thousands and thousands of years ago, beginning with indigenous people, both in North America and in Africa. These beliefs have prevailed through the eons, surviving even when organized religion attempted to turn them around. Native American beliefs today are as wide-ranging as they are firmly planted. African tribal beliefs, just as ancient, also endure; some gave rise to Islam, the second-largest religion in the world after Christianity.

Many afterlife beliefs go back to the first indigenous people who inhabited their land—and they are still embraced by people today. Across the American continents and Africa, many people still practice beliefs that go back thousands of years.

"The spans of the American and African continents are so vast that it's impossible to generalize about their specific religions," said Ken Shouler. One thing that faiths on both continents have in common is that each different tribe possesses—and in some cases still possesses—its spiritual ceremonies and beliefs, even though the spread of missionaries in both Africa and North America did much to diminish the wisdom of these ancient peoples, according to Shouler.

Nevertheless, the roots of many modern beliefs are rooted in the beliefs of these ancient cultures. And many of them are not incompatible with modern religious belief.

The Reverend Damian Milliken, who has been a missionary in Africa since 1960, said the tribal beliefs he was exposed to there helped enhance his spirituality. He said the people he has lived with in Tanzania for more than fifty-plus years celebrate death the same way they celebrate birth.

HAPPY HUNTING GROUNDS

Literature and Hollywood movies over the last century or so have taught us to believe that Native Americans refer to the afterlife as the "happy hunting grounds." But it's actually something made up by white men.

The first written reference to the "happy hunting grounds," according to many sources, is in 1826's *The Last of the Mohicans* by James Fenimore Cooper: "Why do my brothers mourn? Why do my daughters weep? That a young man has gone to the happy hunting-grounds; that a chief has filled his time with honor?"

The phrase soon became a literary favorite. In *Huck Finn and Tom Sawyer among the Indians*, begun by Mark Twain in 1885 and finished by Lee Nelson in 1968: "Injuns ain't likely to steal your horses on such nights, because if you woke up and managed to kill them and they died in the dark, it was their notion and belief it would always be dark to them in the Happy Hunting Grounds . . . ."

Given that Native Americans speak hundreds of languages, it's now widely accepted that the term is a construct of white people's imaginations and generalizations of Native American culture, and most Native American beliefs are similar to those of the Algonquian, Iroquois, and Cherokee: that the afterlife is an endlessly abundant land of spring and summer.

Closer to home, John Bear Mitchell, a citizen of the Penobscot tribe in Maine and a professor at the University of Maine, said his people have managed to maintain their spiritual beliefs despite the intrusion of organized religion. "Organized religions are very well documented. The documentation is not that old—2,000-plus years. By looking at the time humans have existed in my area— 10,000-plus years—we must understand or believe that a higher spiritual power must exist. Thus, we lived our lives based on spirituality. That spirits exist and we must honor them for providing food, water and rain." He said those beliefs can be controversial, because while they don't make religion irrelevant, the lesson is something different than what's taught by organized religion. So the ancient beliefs don't sit well with the belief systems of religious people.

He explained that the beliefs of Native Americans have been misrepresented over the centuries.

"I think far too often it is popular for nonknowing people to assume that Native Americans have many gods when, in fact, we have one God and many spirits. For example, spirits of the land, of the wind, of the water, of the trees, of the animals . . . . Because of popular media, our cultural beliefs have been grouped and categorized as if all Native Americans have the exact same religious, spiritual beliefs—that is a misrepresentation."

NATIVE AMERICANS

Among the many misconceptions that have become standard belief about Native Americans and their beliefs and spirituality is that they are all the same. Hundreds of different tribes, with different customs, languages, and people, make up the nations of Native Americans who live on North American soil.

"It is almost impossible to characterize Native American religions as a whole because of their amazing diversity," said Ken Shouler. "Knowledge about the development of religion in the Native American tribes is imprecise. In fact, the word 'religion' had no equivalent in any of the 300 Native American languages that existed at the time Columbus arrived on the continent." Despite the diversity of beliefs, some generalizations that can be made, particularly concerning death.

"Birth, marriage, and death do not fit into a universal set of beliefs and rites," according to Shouler. "The various rites are meant to be indulged in by the relatives and the community. However, death is considered a transition, and many outcomes are possible following death. Some believe in reincarnation, others that humans return as ghosts, and others that the spirit goes to another world."

Those beliefs can be appealing to those who are looking for something beyond the Christian heaven/hell concept.

Ian Clark wasn't raised in a religious home, although he was taught about heaven and hell. "We never went to church, though my grandmother on my mother's side was at least somewhat religious, as she had a crucifix hanging in her bedroom. Though I was not raised with these specific beliefs, I do remember that my stepfather (whom I lived with from the age of three until I left for college) was in touch with his Native American heritage, and I did take an interest in learning about their culture and beliefs. Culturally I am open to some Native American concepts," he said. He likes the fact that there are multiple spirits. He said part of that appeal is that he doesn't believe that religion has to be specific, and most people worship the same thing without even realizing it.

John Bear Mitchell, the Penobscot citizen, said that while Native American beliefs are wide-ranging and can't all be categorized in one specific belief set, they are also compatible with other religious beliefs. According to him, it boils down to this, "I believe you walk the good road (the hard right way) or you walk the bad road (the easy wrong way). By this, you maintain a direction and you will continue this direction in the afterlife."

John's Story

John describes Wabanaki beliefs this way: "It is taught that there is no hell—instead, when we die, we begin a journey. That journey only begins when the living eat for us. The death feast is the catalyst for when we begin that journey into the afterlife.

WHAT IS WABANAKI?

The Wabanaki confederacy is made up of four tribes that comprise most of the Native American population in the far northeast of the United States and southeast corner of Canada. These tribes include the Passamaquoddy, Penobscot, Mi'kmaq, and Maliseet. Wabanaki means "People of the Dawn." And they truly are—the first place on the continental United States that the rising sun shines is the far eastern coast of Maine, which has the largest population of these tribes. In the 2010 US census, there were 7,900 Native Americans in Maine, which has a population a little more than 1,000,000.

"Here is the short version of how that journey begins.

"Once we die, our spirit leaves the body but only ventures outside the center of our chest. Our spirit will 'float' there until we are put into the earth. Immediately before our body is covered with dirt, the elder allows our spirit to enter the spirit world. However, once we enter the spirit world—our journey doesn't begin until the living hold a feast where they set a plate of food at a table for the deceased. The feast will contain only foods that are native to our land. The food is also usually food that we enjoyed in life, after all, the living are helping the deceased, so what better way to do that than eat the favorite foods of the deceased? Everyone present at the death feast eats his first course (plate) of food in complete silence so as not to attract spirits that may be 'wandering' by. Once the first course is eaten, the plate that was set for the deceased and a glass of water are taken into the forest and laid on the ground, and an offering of tobacco is laid with it. Now the spirit journey begins.

"The spirit now embarks on a yearlong journey. This journey is not easy and is self-guided. Where is the spirit going? No one knows—including the spirit. If the deceased has lived a good life, he will be given guidance by the ones whose job it is to guide them. If the deceased has lived a life fraught with hate and self-greed, then he will receive no guidance but have the same chance to reach the end of the yearlong journey in a good way. However, if that spirit gets lost, he may end up in a swamp, where he becomes mired in mud with no chance of escape, and there—that spirit slowly is consumed by the swamp and will eventually disintegrate and fail to maintain existence. That spirit dies.

"The spirit who has led a good life continues on that yearlong journey. With guidance from the living, the spirit is fueled by water and food that the living periodically consumes for the deceased. At the end of the year, the spirit has a choice. Maintain in the afterlife to help and guide the living by being a protector, or be reborn into the body of an animal. If he remains in the afterlife, he will become available to be a spiritual protector and can assist the living in whatever their good prayers ask for. If he decides to be reborn as an animal, he will serve a purpose to feed the living by giving his mature animal body to the living for food."

AMERICAN INDIAN OR NATIVE AMERICAN?

There is confusion among white people about whether to use the term Indian or the term Native American. Most citizens of tribes will tell you that they prefer to be referred to by their tribe name rather than a generic term, but either term is okay. But some have stronger feelings.

Russell Means, a member of the Lakota tribe who founded the American Indian Movement, wrote in a 1998 essay, "I abhor the term Native American. It is a generic government term used to describe all the indigenous prisoners of the United States . . . . I prefer the term American Indian because I know its origins . . . . We were enslaved as American Indians, we were colonized as American Indians, and we will gain our freedom as American Indians, and then we will call ourselves any damn thing we choose."

The Struggle Continues

The Native American way of life began to take a hit the minute the first white men landed on the North American continent. And with everything else—the loss of land, life, and culture—Christianity played a big part in the dilution and misrepresentation of the spiritual beliefs of American Indians.

"On Native American reservations in the United States, Christianity is often a dirty word," Julia Roller wrote in the article "Native and Christian: A Look at Christianity on Indian Reservations."

She said that many Indians believed that if they became Christian, they were no longer Indians.

The history of Christianity on reservations includes native children who were forced to attend missionary schools, where they were punished for speaking their native language, the only language they knew.

"In hastily erected churches, natives were told they would join the rest of their ancestors in hell if they didn't believe in this white Jesus nailed to a wooden cross in front of them. They were told tales of a God of everlasting love yet punished with a sharp whip for daring to persist in their own traditions," Roller said.

THE MERIAM REPORT

A report published in 1928 for the U.S. government and spear-headed by Lewis Meriam found that Native Americans, who had been forced onto reservations and into poverty, were not thriving, mostly as a result of the government's policies. Among the findings of the report was the fact that the schools created for Native American children, particularly with their emphasis on Christianity, were not working.

The report pointed out that the goal was to convert Indian children to Christianity and give them Christian names, so inheritance of property could be traced and they could be trained to become laborers and household workers. According to *nativeamerican netroots.net*. While the report made abuse of Indian children public, including the fact they were forcibly removed from their homes, it didn't end the official government policy, which continued for another forty years.

The report spurred some changes and reform in the treatment of Native Americans, but many of the hardships for the original inhabitants of the North American continent that are tied to the original treatment by the government continue today.

John Bear Mitchell said that growing up, he was sent to Catholic schools, and it caused a lot of confusion for him. "I was raised in a reservation school that was run by nuns. I was told of hell over and over again, as if to scare me into believing that hell is where you go when you're a bad kid. I guess that was the fear of God," he said. "I was told that hell was full of fire, but as a child who had been surrounded by traditional Native American ceremonies, I was always taught the fire is good—it keeps us warm and cooks our food. This made me question that idea of hell and made me question the values of the nuns as well."

AFRICAN ROOTS

Much like tribal Native American beliefs, African beliefs also can't be tied up into one simple package. "There is no single body of religious dogma for the continent, yet many similarities are found among all the countries," said Ken Shouler. "The simple common denominator is the belief in a single god or creator who is somewhere else. Even though in some instances there is a collection of gods, there is usually one supreme god who has domain over all. These other spiritual beings can be nature spirits and ancestors and are often called the Children of God. Sacrifices to lesser spiritual beings go to the Supreme Being. Many of the religious groups in various parts of the continent are on the decline."

The Emergence of Islam

The largest religious influence in Africa has been Islam. It began in North Africa and eventually spread through much of the continent. Christianity espouses belief in one god, just as Islam espouses belief in one god, Allah. Man's purpose is to worship Allah alone and live a moral life.

Islam spread along the Mediterranean, and was well advanced by the ninth century. Muslim dynasties were established in West Africa as early as the eleventh century. The religion eventually spread across the northern half of the continent.

"People often mistakenly think of African religions as being exclusively concerned with animism, sorcery, and various tribal rituals," Shouler said. Since Africa is divided in two at the Sahara Desert, different beliefs took hold in different places.

While the north of Africa is heavily Islamic, Christianity also made inroads, including in Ethiopia, which is the only African kingdom with a Christian state church. South of the Sahara, there was a heavy influence from Christian missionaries, and much of the continent is Christian.

Shouler said, "In the dense tropical forests, ancient traditional beliefs are still active, except where missionary zeal has made a presence in a country. In those cases, the majority of people have followed the customs and beliefs of the imported religion. Even so, it is highly probable that there has been an intermingling of the traditional with the new."

Islam is the second biggest religion in the world, after Christianity. In the United States, about 2.5 million people are Islamic, according to the 2008 Pew Forum report, although some sources put it as high as 7 million. In the 2008 Pew survey, 77 percent of American Muslims said they believe in an afterlife—just a little higher than the national average. But 67 percent of those said they were "absolutely certain," which is second only to evangelical Christians and Mormons for certainty. The overall average was 50 percent.

Hamid Faizad, 52, who teaches adult education in Maryland, pointed out that Christianity and Islam are actually a lot alike—for instance, he believes in heaven and hell. He said in Islam, "After we die, we go from the grave to judgment day. We are asked questions about God, and if we answer correctly, the doors of paradise are opened. If not, we are punished." He said his belief in the afterlife is simple. "The Koran says so, God said so, and the prophet Mohammed [said so], so it is true."

Religious Belief, and What Does It Mean in America?

As with the indigenous people on our continent, the beliefs of Africans were varied, but had some similarities, including the fact that the earth was created, followed by the animals, and finally the humans.

The intrusion of Europeans diluted and destroyed much of African religious culture. According to Ken Shouler, "Many scholars believe that the African countries that have remained most stable into the twenty-first century are those that retained their traditional ways of life and religions. African religions don't have a dogma consisting of strict religious laws to follow; their entire philosophy is directed to nurturing a proper relationship with the divine and how the divine relates to the earth, life, and community. Their rituals revolve around establishing and maintaining a relationship with the spiritual forces in nature and with the gods. This relationship is accomplished through prayers, offerings, and sacrifices made to shrines and altars."

Shouler said death beliefs are important, and ancestors play an important role in those beliefs, acting as a go-between for spiritual access—to become an ancestor, a person needs to have lived a good, moral life and contributed to the community. Death is not seen as a final stage, as going to a place to be with deceased loved ones. He said much of that ritual and belief has been incorporated into religious practice here in America.

Damian's Story

When the Reverend Damian Milliken went to Tanzania as a young priest fresh from the seminary in 1960, he didn't know what to expect. At the time of our survey, he'd been there for more than fifty years. As a priest, he went to Africa to bring Christianity, specifically Catholicism, to the people. But he doesn't see their beliefs as a contradiction to what he was trying to teach, rather, as an enhancement. Over his many years in Tanzania, he found joy in the way the people he lived among meshed Christian belief with their own.

He said that a story in his book *African Pilgrimage*, which is a compilation of his letters home from Africa, is a great example of that. There had been a bad drought in the village he'd been ministering to. The hoped-for rain coincided with the death of one of the female elders in the region. "Her funeral would be held that day at three in the afternoon. We went up the mountains to the mission where the sister had died and was to be buried after serving fifty years there.

"During the funeral Mass of Sister Sylvester, I wondered how much she had seen and experienced living in this place for more than fifty years; and here she lay in her open coffin, with hundreds of African women, men, and children weeping at her passing.

"At the homily, the pastor struck the right note with the congregation: 'When did Sister Sylvester die?' And the reply came, 'At three o'clock this morning.'

"'And when did the rain start?' And the reply, 'At three o'clock this morning.' And it was the sign to everyone in that church that Sister had truly gone to meet her master, and that she had not forgotten those she left behind.

"I was just a little amused with the simplifications until the Our Father was intoned. In the pause between the intonation and when the congregation could carry on, the church, the coffin, the people and myself began to shake in a minor earthquake. When it was over we continued with fervor, 'Who art in Heaven . . . .'"

In response to our survey, he added, "Africans are very, very concerned with the last moment of life."

He said there is a firm belief that those who have died, like Sister Sylvester, are watching out for those they've left behind, and that you must send them off in the best manner possible.

"The most significant thing is how you die, and everyone wants to be there at the funeral," he said. "No want wants to be absent." The sisters who teach at the school for girls that he built, Saint Mary's Mazinde Juu, are never too busy to attend a funeral. "The termination of life is significant. You are here, and you're not here," said Father Milliken.

He said that there is also a lurking fear of recriminations if a person misses a funeral. "People want to have good omens for the future." He reported that at the funerals he's attended, "No one leaves until the last shovel of dirt is back in the grave. Every scrap of it." The people he lives among definitely believe in an afterlife and also believe their ancestors are aware of what they do in life. The entire ritual is significant; it puts a seal on your life.

As a priest, too, he said he was always moved by the dignity and faith with which most of his parishioners in Tanzania face the end of their life. He tells the story of one woman whom he went to perform last rites on. She was in a little mud hut, covered in a blanket, and she was so far gone she could not even swallow a drop of water.

She had been hiding her hand, but when the priest finally persuaded her to let him see it, he saw she was wearing gold nail polish. She told him she also was expecting to have her hair done. "For when I meet Jesus," she told him.

"For her, it was very simple. There was no moaning or groaning," he says. "She was literally starving to death, but going happily. She knew where she was going and had faith. It moved me."

A passage in his book gives a poignant view of the afterlife. He frequently visited an elderly couple, Veronica and Joseph, in a neighboring village to give them communion and hear their confessions. On one visit, he wrote, "I sat on the bed under the overhang of the grass roof and told them they would sit next to me for their confessions and the receiving of communion. Joseph did so. When he brought Veronica, I could see from her level eye and closed lips that she had determined something other than what I had asked. She left her hold on Joseph and proceeded again to kneel before me. I stood up and took her arms firmly, trying to turn her to sit on the bed.

"She looked at me with the utmost serenity and said with calm determination, 'Baba (Father), I'm not kneeling down for you but for Jesus, whom you have brought to me.'

"When I returned to Ngapa the following month, I was told that we would not have to visit Veronica and Joseph again. They had died shortly after our last call, within days of one another. But we did go, and I said a prayer at that grave in the deserted compound near the spot where Veronica had knelt. I asked for forgiveness and I asked for grace to see what she had seen.

"The cool breeze started and the grass roof of the hut looked ragged. Soon it would be stripped completely. The rains would come and wipe away all trace of Joseph and Veronica's house. The white ants would devour the frame and reed rope of their bed. The frangipani we planted on the grave will probably still be there, though. When we left and walked down the ridge, the mist blotted out the sight of the plateau and left my dear friends on a splendid elevation between earth and heaven.

"I never went back there again, but I often call on the names of Joseph and Veronica to intercede for me."

CHAPTER FIVE

THE DAWNING OF AQUARIUS—AND THE AFTERLIFE

As belief in heaven and hell diminishes, people feel more free to form their own beliefs. Over the past couple decades, many who believe they are spiritual but not necessarily religious have embraced New Age, Wicca, and other nontraditional beliefs, even if academics and religious leaders aren't sold.

Most people tie afterlife beliefs to religion—and for those who practice a religion, they can't imagine it any other way. But for those who have alternative beliefs, an afterlife may be exclusive from religion . . . or go beyond religion . . . or be compatible with religion. In other words, religion may or may not have anything to do with what happens once we die.

While it may seem to some as though alternative beliefs are a modern concept, many are actually tied in to ancient beliefs.

John Griffin, a professor at World University in Ojai, California, said the world has changed and made people more open to different ways of looking at the big question. He believes there are several reasons people are embracing nontraditional religious views. "We have a longer and more objective perspective on history, more people are better educated, educational material is widely available on television and the internet and censorship has diminished as sources of previously unavailable information have increased. America and many other countries have become increasingly pluralistic with more diverse populations and cultural influences. All this combines to allow people to consider other religious options that were previously unknown to them, ignored, or even suppressed."

E. Brooks Holifield, the Emory professor of comparative religions, said nontraditional beliefs are actually nothing new. "The nontraditional views of an afterlife actually began in the early nineteenth century. In the medieval era, people believed that the purpose of the afterlife was to glorify God. By the nineteenth century, the purpose was to be reunited with departed loved ones, and heaven, especially, was domesticated. It was an extension of relationships here," he said.

While most of the respondents to our survey still characterized themselves as having at least a basis in traditional belief, they had also formed their own beliefs that departed from traditional teachings. Holifield said the tendency towards this has been forming for some time, and is seen in the tendency of even clerics to not dwell a lot on hell. "The older idea of a God of wrath tended to fade in the nineteenth century and give way to a more loving conception of God. Some of this was the result of the Enlightenment and its turn to a humanitarian conception of God. Rarely in liberal Protestant or Catholic pulpits do preachers talk about the wrath of God or the danger of hell, and these emphases are also disappearing slowly from evangelical churches. Only in fundamentalist churches and some Pentecostal churches does such language still play an important part in worship or Christian self-understanding.

"Many Christians now tend to interpret the Bible figuratively, and they see both heaven and hell as metaphors that point to mysteries that are not fully within the range of our comprehension.

"Many still believe in an afterlife, but they tend to believe in the Greek concept of the immortality of the soul rather than the New Testament conception of the resurrection of the body (though it is a somewhat strange body that presumably arises).

Actually the New Testament doesn't say much about heaven; it talks of the Kingdom of God. People tend to fit their religion to their own presuppositions, especially when [the presuppositions] are comforting," he concluded.

According to Shouler, a lot of the changes in belief have to do more with pseudo-science than religious thought. "With all the advances in science and technology, so many Americans still embrace pseudo-science. I don't think the ever-present love of pseudo-science can be ignored in (the Afterlife Survey). People accept astrology, believe in angels (hence the popularity of TV shows with angels in the title), believe in a sports zone (which I have lectured on), believe in the paranormal, are fundamentalists concerning religious texts, and so on."

He added that metaphysics is "wide open, with no penalties for believing in unprovable things."

Many New Age, Wiccan, and other nontraditional afterlife beliefs center around metaphysics, which is the study of the basic nature of being.

Therefore, "The issues surrounding god, the soul, eternal life, ghosts, and other spirits remain . . . 'open' questions. Who can disprove anyone in this realm?"

Whatever the reason is behind the change, it's caught on. "New Age beliefs share common ground: seeking respect from the traditional religions just as they, in turn, respect the beliefs of those people," said Shouler. "Many New Age followers belong to an existing religion, with the New Age philosophy as an adjunct to their central beliefs. Other members have discarded the religion they were born into in favor of a more free-flowing, nondogmatic belief. New Age spirituality has no holy text, clergy, or creed."

He said the disillusionment people began to have with established religions, government, and other institutions probably had a lot to do with people forming their own beliefs. "It is certainly a spiritual movement, a veritable mélange of beliefs borrowed from existing faiths."

And, whatever the motivation, it takes the best of the ancient beliefs, something that may appeal to those who find organized religion too stifling.

The central belief of the New Age movement is that everyone is part of one, interdependent whole. It embraces unity beyond all beliefs, loves all living things, and doesn't embrace personal judgment of others.

NEW AGE AND MORE

There are a variety of different beliefs that can come under the "New Age" heading. There is New Age itself, which has a specific set of beliefs. But there are also offshoots, like Wicca, which many see as "witchcraft," but is actually a belief system based on connection to the earth and the world around us. Two of our survey responders are Wiccan priestesses.

There are also Zen, spiritualism, spiritism, Scientology, and secularism, among others.

Here are some of the most popular:

Wicca

Rooted in ancient Celtic pagan belief, Arin Murphy-Hiscock described Wicca as "a single stream of alternative spirituality within the larger field of earth-based spiritualities classified as pagan or neopagan."

Wiccan belief today merges many beliefs, including ancient Celtic and "deity structure, and seasonal days of celebration with modern material from ceremonial magic," Ken Shouler said.

The modern Wiccan movement dates back to England during the 1950s and quickly spread to the United States, with around 750,000 adherents nationwide.

Those who practice Wicca follow an ethical code called Wiccan Rede, which maintains that whatever they do comes back to them threefold. Therefore, if they harm, they get harm back to the power of three. "Therefore, they have no incentive to curse anyone; the curse would come back to haunt them three times over," said Shouler. "Witches may practice some form of ritual magic, which must be considered 'good magic.' Their ethical code is spelled out in the saying: 'An' it harm none, do what thou wilt.'" Which is very similar to the ancient Jainism saying "You are that which you wish to harm."

According to the American Council of Witches, "A witch seeks to control forces within her/himself that make life possible in order to live wisely and well, without harm to others, and in harmony with nature." Wiccans also have deep respect for the environment and value femininity. Their deity is a god or goddess, which is the same God that others worship, just more relatable as a mother or father figure.

Scientology

Scientology, developed by L. Ron Hubbard after he wrote *Dianetics: The Modern Science of Mental Health,* in 1950, claims that a person needs to "get clear" by a process called "auditing." When people go through audits, they get rid of the experiences in their lives that block self-realization. The religion doesn't have a specific afterlife belief, but maintains that during an audit, a person can examine things that happened in a past life, which would mean that one can live multiple lives.

Spiritualism
This is a belief that spirits—or a force that isn't necessarily God—is at work in the universe. It comes from a mix of ancient beliefs.

Spiritism
Those who practice spiritism believe that spirits are present here on earth and that humans can make contact with them.

Secular Humanism, or Humanism
Humanists believe that human reasoning is what makes us who we are, and they reject religion and all other supernatural beliefs. The belief system maintains that humans alone are responsible for their lives and well-being; that they are not superior to nature, but must live with it. It also maintains that nothing should be taken on faith, but that people need to make reasoned decisions about the world around them based on what they learn.

Kabbalah
In recent years, many celebrities, most notably the pop star Madonna, have embraced Kabbalah. So is it the real deal or a religious fad?

The belief system, which comes from Jewish mystic belief, holds that everything in a person's life—health, relationships, business—comes from the same root. Studying Kabbalah doesn't require you to leave your current faith or religious path. Kabbalah teaches universal principles that apply to people of all faiths and all religions, regardless of ethnicity or background. Kabbalah's goal is to help people deepen their understanding of the universe and to give them the tools to understand why things are happening and how to connect to the light of the creator to find fulfillment.

Sounds great, right? So why is it treated with such derision? Writer Daphne Merkin, in an article for the *New York Times Magazine*, set out to get to the bottom of it. Upon a visit to the Kabbalah Centre in Los Angeles, which is the epicenter of the U.S. Kabbalah craze, Merkin said, "Although the center denies its association with Judaism or any other existing religion . . . its tiny insider circle of members (numbering a bit more than 200 in all), referred to as the *chevra*, or group of friends, abide by the laws and customs that are the underpinning of observant Judaism."

Merkin also recounts an interview she had with Madonna, probably the world's most famous Kabbalah practitioner, who told her she liked Kabbalah because the thought of eternal life appealed to her. Madonna told her that she doesn't think people's energy just disappears.

Merkin wrote, "When I asked her why she hadn't stuck with Catholicism, which incorporates belief in an afterlife, she snapped in reply: 'There's nothing consoling about being Catholic. They're all just laws and prohibitions. They don't help me negotiate the world.'"

Merkin, whose mother died of cancer before her visit to the Kabbalah Centre, concluded that the movement raises more questions than it answers. She added, "Here's what I do know: My mother has shown no signs thus far of resurfacing, and I would guess that Madonna continues to believe in her own immortality, as guaranteed by the center."

When asked about Kabbalah, Rabbi Ilene Schneider, an Afterlife Survey participant, added this thought, "The true study of Kabbalah is not a trendy New Age fad, but a deep contemplation of the mysteries of the divine, creation, the universe and our place in it."

THE WICCAN WAY

Two of the respondents to our survey are Wiccan, and while they share a basic philosophy, their beliefs differ. Which they say is just natural—Wiccan beliefs *will* differ. Here are their stories.

Arin Murphy-Hiscock

Murphy-Hiscock, who has been a practicing pagan Wiccan priestess for fifteen years and has written several books on the topic, explains the general philosophy behind Wiccan afterlife beliefs this way: "Most believe in some form of continuing process, generally a re-initiation of the cycle in the form of reincarnation. Between incarnations, the soul resides in what is often referred to as the Summerland. The Summerland is not the pagan equivalent of heaven; it is not a reward, a place of judgment, or a permanent state, but a place of temporary rest and rejuvenation where the soul can look back on its recent incarnation and evaluate its experiences before moving on to its next incarnation. As the length of stay in the Summerland varies for each spirit's requirements for rest and reflection, it is entirely possible the spirits who knew one another in a past incarnation will meet one another there. Different paths within the pagan classification may call this place by different names, although the Summerland seems to be among the most popular terms. When a soul has finished its cycle of incarnations (and the number of cycles can vary according to the spirit's needs and experiences) it is theorized that there is another plane of existence beyond the Summerland to which the spirit can move, sometimes considered union with the energy of the divine, a return to the energy that created the universe."

Of her own beliefs, she says, "To be honest, I have no concrete expectations. I have taught my young son about the Summerland as he encounters death of pets or characters in books, and he finds it comforting. I expect there to be a continuing cycle of existence in some form, but I think to make an assumption about what it will be would be limiting. I find the concept of the Summerland, a place/time where my spirit can reflect upon its experiences and the lessons it has learned before beginning its next cycle of existence, to be a very open one and I am comfortable with that."

She also pointed out, "In pagan practices and systems, more importance is placed on the here and now as opposed to a goal-oriented afterlife. More suffering now does not indicate a reward for patience or forbearance down the line; good fortune is not a sign of favor. We are responsible for our actions in this life, and for the lessons learned, and the consequences must be dealt with here and now. Ultimately, the soul will have the opportunity to reflect upon its experiences and the issues encountered in this life once it has passed from this incarnation, and understanding will be achieved to some extent, if it is not achieved during the present incarnation."

Ashleen O'Gaea

Ashleen O'Gaea is a Wiccan priestess and author of both fiction and nonfiction books.

She said, "None of us can speak for all of us, but the broadest way I can put it is that our souls are carried by the Goddess' unconditional love to the Summerland—known by various names, including the Land of Youth—where we have an opportunity to learn from the joys and challenges of the life just lived before the God guides us back to another incarnation. How exactly this happens, and when, has to do with an individual's belief.

"How we imagine the Summerland—how we imagine the Goddess and God!—and how we understand the idea of learning from our previous lives are all full of possibilities. I know one or two Wiccans who are sure that not reincarnating is an option, and trust that this does not mean they aren't Wiccan. As far as I know and personally believe, though, a belief that we'll take up a permanent residence in some otherworldly estate is beyond the parameters of Wicca.

She said that she has seen people's perceptions of an afterlife change when they embrace Wicca.

"Given that some Wiccans have come from punishing-deity faiths, I hope their understandings change. Wicca acknowledges that what we do has consequences, and that we are responsible—able to respond—rather than just to blame. My tradition, at least, teaches that reincarnation isn't something that happens 'till you get it right,' but that it's just 'how life works.' We may need a chance to practice new approaches, but when that's true, it's just another reason to celebrate the process. The experience of joy is always the emphasis."

When asked what she thinks causes some people's view of the afterlife to change, she said, "Sometimes it's as simple as becoming aware that there's another way of looking at it than the way we were initially taught. Sometimes it's an experience that sets us wondering whether what we've always thought is really how things go. I think there's usually more than one factor at work when people make radical changes in their beliefs."

And why does all this matter?

"My tradition teaches that the reason we're alive is to be—and that death is another step in the spiral dance of life. The music doesn't stop when we die, so we keep dancing, and I think that matters because it means that the dance and our steps in it are important. Generally speaking, the Wiccan afterlife is not one that inspires avoidance. I think it inspires confidence; I find it comforting that my soul can learn, not just from mistakes, but from successes as well. Wicca is, after all, an experiential religion, and in our mundane Western lives we're beginning to favor virtual experience over physical, person-to-person activity. As Wiccans, we don't have to depend wholly on the afterlife to return us to that experiential source of authentic holiness, but that's what our afterlife is, and I think it's very important."

THE METAPHYSICAL APPROACH: KENDRA VAUGHN HOVEY

Most New Age belief has a lot to do with metaphysics, which is the study of being.

Kendra Vaughn Hovey has a PhD from the American Institute of Holistic Theology as well as a doctor of ministry from the University of Metaphysics, so her beliefs are something she has thought about quite a bit. She was raised in a Jewish household, was once a Wiccan priestess, and also once held devout Christian beliefs. As a pagan minister, she believes in God. While metaphysics is a general and wide-ranging concept, so is paganism. It refers to any religion or belief system that doesn't believe in one God. Therefore, both concepts cover a lot of areas in New Age belief.

"I personally believe that God is energy or spirit," she said "As such, we live by the laws of natural order that govern the universe and never change (e.g., gravity). Knowing God as energy, there is no doubt in my mind that when I die, my spirit will unite with the spirit of God and I will be at peace and at rest. Whether or not I will remain there or reincarnate, I do not know. I do believe, though, that I will know all spirits and all spirits will know me."

Not only does she believe in an afterlife, but, "In fact I don't know anyone who doesn't. Although, I do not think that all New Agers/pagans view the afterlife exactly the same. One of the beautiful things about being a practitioner of metaphysics is that we know the mind is very powerful—it would have to be in order to be a part of the great universal mind. That being said, isn't it conceivable that the afterlife will be exactly as each person envisions it? Possibly.

"I think in a Western world our frame of reference is Western religious thought, which includes the belief of both heaven and hell. But that is certainly not the case worldwide or with the New Age and pagan community of the Western world. It is safe to say that New Agers and pagans only believe in some form of heaven and reject the belief in hell altogether."

She said she doesn't believe in hell. "Another fascinating point is that early Christians did not believe in hell either. That belief did not come into existence until, I believe, Augustine's day. Perhaps it was because of the pagan and/or Jewish influence of the people at that time.

> ### NEW AGE FOR EVERYONE
> According to the Pew Forum survey, about one quarter of those who responded, no matter what their religious beliefs, also believe some things associated with New Age religions, including that there is spiritual energy in things like mountains and trees (26%), that the position of the stars—astrology—can have an affect on a person's life (25%), and that yoga is not just an exercise, but a spiritual practice (23%). Some also believe in something definitely not New Agey—that a person can curse another person or cast the "evil eye" on them (16%).

As far as thoughts of an afterlife go, she added, "Why worry ourselves with such things? Metaphysics teaches us that so long as we are aligned with the love of God, we can shape and create our world the way we want it. I think it is time for pagans (or those who believe in karma) and Christians (or those who believe in the devil) to stop blaming their circumstances on things that are outside of themselves and start changing their life's circumstances into what they want without excuses. I think forgiving others but also forgiving ourselves, as God has forgiven us, is the first step in making positive change in our lives."

NEW AGE OR NEW ARGH? THE ACADEMICS SPEAK

While New Age beliefs have grown more and more popular, many dismiss them as feel-good pseudo-religion without a lot of substance. But John Griffin, the World University professor, said criticisms of New Age beliefs come from a failure to look at the big picture. "I could quote Ecclesiastes 1:9, 'There is nothing new under the sun.' There is some truth to this that is applicable to this question. Traditional and nontraditional beliefs represent cobbled-together concepts if you trace the context of their derivations. This is usually a good thing, as it is the way human knowledge builds and grows."

He said that while Christianity owes a debt to Judaism, which itself borrowed from other cultures, Christianity also took concepts from Platonism and hermeticism to form its beliefs.

He added that the wide availability of information allows people to form their beliefs.

"People also generally have more time to think and have longer life spans and retirement time. Heaven is no longer thought of as a place high in the sky, as we now know a considerable amount about other planets, galaxies, and the staggering extent of the universe itself. Heaven and hell are now often thought of as states of mind and/or other dimensional states. The concept of reincarnation (which was an option in early Christianity before a church council discouraged the belief) and the huge number of near-death experience testimonies from around the world have contributed to our thoughts about heaven and hell."

The Other View

Andrew Gurevich, a professor of philosophy and literature at Mount Hood Community College in Gresham, Oregon, has a different take on what New Age beliefs mean in modern-day

America, and what this says about Americans as a society. He believes the answer is a complex one.

"The great postwar religious revival that saw church attendance skyrocket in the 1940s and 1950s came at the expense of traditional doctrine and content according to many sociologists and theologians," he said when we asked him to explain the growing popularity of New Age beliefs. He said scholars Will Herberg, in 1955, and Stephen Prothero have both addressed the subject of American consumer culture and how it was beginning to define religion.

He said the whole point is that while making religion appeal to the masses, American religious traditions have become "so empty and content-less, so conformist, so utilitarian, so sentimental, so individualistic, and so self-righteous that they no longer effectively teach the more complex and troubling doctrines to their 'customers.'"

He said that Ed Bernays, the nephew of Sigmund Freud, was the creator of the public relations and modern advertising movements in the United States. Bernays realized you could manipulate the masses by appealing to their subconscious, irrational desires and then combining that with fear and greed. "I see complete parallels between all of this, and the modern view of the afterlife as a sort of twenty-four-hour Mall of America," said Gurevich.

"On the other side of this equation, we seem to have an opposing force that ironically drives many people to the same sorts of conclusions. In other words, the evident demise of access to the American dream is replaced by the innocuous, ill-defined dream of a better life in the world to come. This fits tendencies of New Age universalism, too. It is the culmination of the push towards private religion, the 'me' generation, and the notion of God as self. We have been socially engineered to seek after our own desires. . . . Americans since the 1960s have become increasing emboldened as they shop for metaphysical systems and views of the afterlife that best suit their individual desires. My Christian neighbors in the Pacific Northwest, for example, are convinced that the heavenly banquet will certainly include organic vegetables and grass-fed beef."

PART TWO
The People's Afterlife—
What Do We Really Believe?

While afterlife beliefs cover a wide range of religious, spiritual, and cultural ground, there is a lot more to it than what happens to us after we die. Death and beliefs that surround it are such an integral part of life, whether a person believes in an afterlife or not, so these beliefs have a big impact on many other aspects of life. They inform how people deal with the details surrounding death or dying, how we relate to our pets, and how we relate to each other. They also have an impact on how we live our lives and how we see the world around us.

CHAPTER SIX

LIFE SUCKS—OR DOESN'T.
AND THEN YOU DIE

Skeptics are a tough sell in any afterlife debate. From those whose religious beliefs don't support an afterlife to atheists who don't believe in God or an afterlife, they are in the minority. They even find themselves under attack from those who do believe. What's behind this point of view?

You live. You die. That's it.

Most people don't like to think about that. But there are those in our survey who, whether they think about it much or not much at all, believe there's simply no afterlife. Some are more sure of that than others.

As much as religion is tied to belief in an afterlife, lack or religion doesn't necessary mean unbelief: Some 10 percent of atheists in the Pew survey said they may not believe in God, but they still believe in an afterlife.

And there are several religions—Judaism, Jehovah's Witnesses, and to a lesser extent, Buddhism and Hinduism—that don't hinge on an afterlife. In the Pew survey, 45 percent of both Jews and Jehovah's Witnesses interviewed didn't believe in an afterlife.

Poet Billy Collins wonders what the nonexistence of an afterlife means, and whether people are ready to face that. "Well, if something 'happens' to you after you die, then you don't really die, do you? We create heaven because it's easier [to comprehend] than the void. For those who need to be reminded of death's finality, I recommend Philip Larkin's poem 'Aubade,' which contains not-so-consoling lines such as 'Many things won't happen. This one will' and 'Nothing more terrible, nothing more true.'"

Rabbi Ilene Schneider knows the feeling. "Rationally, I believe that when you're dead, you're dead," she said. "But emotionally, it is comforting to believe that this life isn't all there is."

And that's the crux of it, say the experts. People need to believe.

WHO ARE JEHOVAH'S WITNESSES?

Jehovah's Witnesses are followers of a relatively new religion, founded in the United States in the 1870s, that bases its beliefs on a strict reading of the Bible. The religion has its own version of the Bible, *The New World Translation of the Holy Scriptures,* and requires its adherents to follow only that version. They believe in an afterlife to the extent that Armageddon will come, and 144,000 people will help to rule over the earth, with God as the final arbiter of who is among that number. They don't celebrate holidays such as Christmas or birthdays. In 2010 the organization reported it had 7.2 million members in the United States. The 2008 Pew survey indicated that only 37 percent of those raised as a Jehovah's Witness stayed in the religion.

"What does this prove?" asked Ken Shouler, in response to the Pew survey finding that 74 percent of Americans believe in an afterlife. "A majority of people in America believe in angels. So in general, people have no problem accepting one kind of mythology or another. My question occurs further upstream: What does it prove? Even if 74 percent do believe, that would be a version of the *ad populum* fallacy (i.e., claiming some statement is true because a majority believes it is). Majorities once thought that the earth was flat and accepted the geocentric hypothesis. So what?"

Skeptics throughout history have wavered about what lack of an afterlife really means. Those who responded to the Afterlife Survey were no different.

WHAT DOES "NO AFTERLIFE" MEAN?

While the answer to "What would no afterlife be?" may seem like a simple question, it's actually not. For instance —is it "nothing?" Or is there something there? And if there is, how can it not exist?

While there are religions that reject the idea of an afterlife, most people tie the belief to a lack of belief in God. So we'll take a look at that.

WHAT IS ATHEISM?

Atheism is the view that there is no divine being, no God. According to Shouler, this statement is the bone of contention between believers and nonbelievers. However, it is not just the existence or nonexistence of God that is disputed. Both sides of the issue know that the existence of God implies the existence of divine providence and the possibility of divine intervention in the world. Theists embrace a belief in this kind of active God. Such a God is a loving being and even answers prayers. When opponents voice an objection to this view of God, they aren't necessarily doubting the existence of God; they're disputing the being's caring nature. This opposing view isn't atheism, strictly speaking, but antitheism.

But, said Shouler, atheists believe "that gods do not or God does not exist. Also, the disbelief in any kind of supernatural existence that is supposed to affect the universe."

Michael Hawkins, 26, a Maine college biology student, and one of the youngest respondents to our survey, puts himself firmly in the camp of the atheists.

"Atheism is consistently misrepresented," he said. "Many people believe it is a positive claim that says there is no God. For all intents and purposes, that is the rhetoric of atheism, but it is not the belief of the vast majority of atheists. Instead we say there is no evidence for any gods and we therefore believe it is extremely unlikely there is one. It is much like any other mythical creature. Sure, there could be unicorns, but there is no evidence for them and it is unlikely they exist. It isn't up to atheists to disprove them."

He said frustration at how uninformed others were is what drove him to research God and the origins of the universe, and that's what began to inform his opinion.

"In high school I had dinner with a friend, his mother, and two of his mother's young Earth creationist friends. At the time I was not well-versed in science, but I did know that the Earth and universe were well into the millions, perhaps billions, of years in age. However, the two creationists in the room discussed how the Earth was seven thousand years old. I knew they were wrong, but I didn't know by exactly how much or exactly why. I would later look it up, finding the Earth was 4.5-plus billion years old. It seemed the creationists were off a bit," he said. For instance, one common creationist belief is that the Earth was created in 4004 B.C.

"This started me on a quest to find out the basic answers about the universe and, specifically, the history of life. I wanted to know how evolution worked and why creationists had a habit of saying so many wrong things all the time. Eventually I turned my attention to evolution specifically because of its importance to our entire history. I am now a major in biology and will be attending grad school somewhere within the field."

He added that atheism is misunderstood: "Atheists are one of the most discriminated-against groups in the nation. Recent polls show that Americans would be more likely to vote Muslims and gays into office than they would atheists. It is assumed that atheists are immoral because they do not use god as a basis for morality. But neither did most enlightenment thinkers. Indeed, nor do most people today. Instead people apply their own ideas of right and wrong to given situations, often appealing to reason in some form. In fact, no religion has every moral situation covered yet people still make moral decisions. Whatever their basis [of these decisions], it isn't religion and it isn't any god." A case in point when it comes to the misunderstanding of atheism can be seen in the exuberant response of Jim Robidoux, the sheet-metal worker who is a fundamentalist Christian, when asked to comment on atheism.

"THE MOST HATED WOMAN IN AMERICA"

One of the most famous atheists in America over the last fifty years was Madalyn Murray O'Hair. Her lawsuit, Murray vs. Curlett, was instrumental in the 1963 Supreme Court ruling that prayer should not be mandated in public schools. In 1964, *Life* magazine described her as "the most hated woman in America." Of the afterlife, O'Hair, who was notoriously blunt, told the Society of Separationists in Austin, Texas, in 1966: "I am neither afraid or ashamed to say what I believe or what I think. I am an atheist and this means at least that I do not believe there is a god or any god, personal or in nature or manifesting himself or itself in any way. I do not believe there is such a thing as heaven or hell or perdition or any of the stages in between. I do not believe there is life after death." Her statement on atheism that was included with her court case elaborated: "An atheist believes that heaven is something for which we should work now—here on earth for all men together to enjoy."

O'Hair founded the American Atheists. She and her son and granddaughter were murdered by a member of the group in 1995.

"Atheism is crazy!!!," he responded in the survey. "The only reason to be an atheist is to live your life as though you were God. You can make all the rules once God is out of the way. Be your own God, you decide what's right and wrong. Good luck with that."

But Michael Hawkins sees the whole issue from an entirely different angle.

"I once considered myself an agnostic," he said. (An agnostic believes that the existence of God can't be known, while an atheist believes that because it can't be proved, there is no God.) "I believed a decision could not be made one way or the other, therefore a position of neutrality was necessary. However, I would later learn that it isn't up to me to disprove God in order to disbelieve in him/her/it."

In the Afterlife Survey, those respondents who do not believe in an afterlife had as varied a view as those who do, from firm *disbelievers* to those who felt firm, but still wondered, to those who believed we don't go on but there are still "afterlives."

AFTER THIS COMES . . . NOTHING

Some of the most certain responders to our survey are those who believe there is no afterlife. This includes both those who describe themselves as atheists and those who don't.

"There is no afterlife, since neither the evidence of the senses, nor that of the intellect supports it," said Ken Shouler. "Camus said life was absurd, in the sense that we are here, we die, and that's it. We give it meaning with our projects and pursuits. We had better get on with these," he said, "since nothing follows."

Martin Scattergood, 53, an engineer and company owner, agrees, vehemently. "I have recently lost my niece to cancer," he said. "I attended her funeral and thought and continue to think about her. In some way, through my memory, she continues to exist, but I do not consider this as an afterlife. It is only in my head. I believe death is finality," he said. "Therefore, we should focus on living and enjoy life."

But Scattergood said he does not consider himself an atheist. "I do not believe in a god," he said. "However, I do consider myself to uphold spiritual/religious values without worship. I am not able to relate to religion, and it probably derives from being forced to attend Sunday school as a child."

And, like the others who don't believe in an afterlife, he said, "I believe that only our deeds, actions, and experiences during living can give meaning to our lives."

Michael Hawkins said his position is black and white. "I am an atheist. While it is rhetorically popular to characterize my position as religious, I, in fact, have no religion. I have taken a default position that can only be changed with evidence—the onus is on the believer. So far no one has presented a bit of evidence.

"Once I die that is the end of me. I do not continue to think or believe or feel or do anything else characteristic of life. The basis of my life is my genes and environment working in concert to produce a functional biological organism; the root of my humanity is exposed through the brain. Once the brain ends, and certainly once all the biology of my being ends, there is nothing. It will be remarkable similar to the time prior to my existence. I just won't know it."

Michael said he was raised with traditional Catholic beliefs, but once he started thinking for himself, he started questioning those beliefs.

"I was raised going to a Catholic school. My home life was not especially religious, but I was raised to believe that there is an eternal afterlife and its quality depends upon what one does over a roughly eighty-year period. I only started questioning it once I left my Catholic school and was exposed to the wildly incorrect views of creationists in high school. That started me down a path of science which crossed into more contradictory religious ideas."

And Mark Henderson, the pastor-turned-atheist who has been told his cancer is terminal, said he's at peace with this life "even though I hold no belief in an afterlife whatsoever."

His father was a funeral director, and Mark said, "I've always said that the greatest gift my father gave me was a 'familiarity' with death. When family members died (several close ones in my youth) I was never shuffled off to one side, but was included in everything. When his father died (on my fifteenth birthday) he didn't ask me about it, he just took me for a little private 'viewing,' just the three of us. It was a powerful and helpful upbringing, especially, as it turned out, I was called on to officiate at my first funeral on my nineteenth birthday. So from a relatively young age I had *not* only had reason to consider this subject on a personal level, but on a professional level, too. The older I've gotten, the more reason I've found not to be so bored with this life that the prospect of a next holds much appeal. There is so much richness and beauty present in this life that it's almost seemed unapprecia-tive to hope for 'something better' in a next life."

And now that he faces terminal cancer, his belief is stronger than ever.

"I don't think I'm going to come down to end and have some terrible sense of panic that I can't let go," he said. A few weeks before the survey, he was in such bad shape, his wife was told his death was imminent. He said it didn't make him rethink his views on an afterlife. "All I felt was I need to find the toehold, the grab bar to keep me going." (Read more of Mark's story in Chapter 12.)

BELIEVERS CAN'T BELIEVE IT

As diverse as their views may be, those who have a solid belief system about the spiritual world and what happens in the afterlife also are solidly against the belief that there is no God and nothing after death.

Jim Robidoux, the sheet-metal worker, said that in the end, "God judges us all." But he added, "Christ himself stands at the door and knocks. If we answer the door, he promises to come in. He also promises he will never leave or forsake us; he will be there with us till the end of time. I've been told masterpieces have been painted of Jesus standing at the door and knocking. The door he stands at has no handle. He cannot open the door. You have to open the door, he will not."

And John Bear Mitchell of the Penobscot tribe said that the belief in no afterlife "is not in our teachings." He said, "[it goes] against everything we learn about or work for in our lives."

Added Brian McHugh, the funeral director, "I feel very sorry for people who live their lives believing that what they see around them is all there is."

And he said, as someone who deals with families facing death every day, "I often wonder how someone can not believe in an afterlife and ever really heal after attending their child's funeral."

THERE IS NO AFTERLIFE . . . KIND OF

Elizabeth Daniels, 26, the executive assistant/office manager, believes, "When people die—that's it—they're dead."

"I only know the facts that are in my face, so there is no way of me knowing or trying to claim that I know what will happen to myself or anyone else after death. An afterlife is certainly as possible as some of the other religious beliefs that I've heard of. Then again, I don't grasp many, if any, of these popular beliefs. To me, being realistic and educated does not leave much room for being religious."

John Reed, the high school teacher, agreed that death is death, but there are no hard and fast rules. "Physically, I think you just die," he said. "I've always imagined it like the light in the old TV tube, how the picture just reduced to that tiny white spot, then it blinked out. I'm afraid of that blinking, but that's what I think happens."

But he added, "I believe people live on in others' memories. So long as we continue to have an effect through that memory, we have an 'afterlife.'"

He said that studying literature and writing stories of his own "has led me to understand that we are a symbolic species, and we share many of our symbols across societies and times and places . . . I see so many people wish so hard for something to be true, and fall for so many tricks like Jonathan Edwards talking to the dead. The afterlife is a symbol of all our hopes, dreams, and vindictiveness, and we wish it to be real, so for many people, it is."

He said belief in God is similar, quoting Joseph Campbell, "There is one truth, but the sages speak of it by many names." John added, "I think truth is goodness, and love, and ethics, and happiness. I think all of the mythologies and holy books preach that. In that regard, I believe in them all. But I think they are all metaphors for the much-too-abstract ideas of love and goodness, and that societies have gotten so lost in the metaphors, they came to think they were the real thing."

John's also a published writer. "I love reading and writing ghost stories. I like the idea that my dead loved ones are 'looking down on me' and that they care about how I am doing. But I also know that that is my sentimental side coming through. It comes down to whether I am honoring their memory and the efforts they made to make me the person I am. I wasn't born 'for a reason,' but now that I'm here, I have a duty to my forebears (family, literary, ethically) to do the best I can with what they left behind."

Rabbi Ilene Schneider agrees that death gives life meaning, "Only if we live a good life here and have left a [meaningful] legacy for those we've influenced while alive."

Even those who don't practice alternative beliefs have a looser view of an afterlife and what it may mean—different from the strict heaven-and-hell concept they may have been taught as children. Many of our survey respondents, even many of those who consider themselves traditionally religious, waver on exactly what happens after death.

Brian McHugh, the funeral director and a practicing Catholic, said, "The more I see people struggle to understand why their loved one has left this life, the more I appreciate and comprehend why humans should believe in an afterlife, be it the traditional heaven and hell or some other variation more suitable to their own beliefs."

And Scott Moulton, the investment services manager who once believed in the traditional heaven and hell, said, "As I move farther and farther away from a traditional belief in heaven and hell, I have moved towards a belief in the concept that the universe itself may be alive and we may be but a subset of a much larger consciousness—much like our bodies are made up of individual living cells that live and die, independent of our larger consciousness or spirit."

Andrew Gurevich, professor of philosophy and literature, said, "There are a few ways to answer this question. In one sense it is a contradiction, in another it isn't."

"I am reminded of the fundamental paradox lying at the heart of most modern American belief systems: the high-in-sentimentality, low-in-rationality assumption that by simply believing in something it makes it 'true for you.' Even skeptics and atheists are prone to this blind spot.

"In a cynical construction, I would suggest that the fear of our own animality—our essential, material death—coupled with the deeply engrained sense of the importance (and permanence) of the self perpetuated by this culture have left most of us existentially handicapped. We are victims to the ravages of time and enslaved by the shackles of history. We simply cannot imagine anything else. So before we even begin, we are at a disadvantage. We have somehow removed ourselves from the natural experience of time and thus severed our intuitive connection to the cosmos. All religion seeks to first explain how this rupture occurred, and subsequently how to reestablish the connection. The word 'religion' itself comes from the Latin for 'to tie back,' or 'tie together.'

"In speaking of heaven, C. S. Lewis once wisely noted that to a child who imagines chocolate as the greatest of all potentiality, heaven must be a place filled with chocolate. It follows then that to a mature adult who is contemplating what seems to them to be the infinitely valuable nature of existence and consciousness, these elements 'must' somehow figure into the fabric of eternity. Also, we come at this from the standpoint of already experiencing this consciousness in a limited sense, so the notion of evolving or growing towards nonexistence is difficult, if not impossible, to fully embrace."

IF NOTHING'S THERE, WHAT IS THERE?

But Gurevich said that many who say they don't believe in an afterlife are still confused about the issue. The concept reminds him of a Hindu proverb: A wealthy man decides to renounce everything to seek liberation. He leaves his wealth, family, and social obligations and lives in a simple hut with nothing more than a begging bowl, a shawl, and a copy of the Vedas. After six months, nothing happens. One day an elderly *sannyasin* is passing by, and the man asks him, "I have renounced all of my wealth, family, and social status to seek enlightenment, and nothing has happened. What must I do?"

To this the monk simply replies, "You must renounce all you have," and walks on. The man is puzzled and thinks, "All I have left is this simple hut. Well, so be it . . . " and he destroys the hut and lives completely exposed to the extremes of nature.

Six months pass and still nothing happens. Again the sage walks by. Frustrated, the man approaches again and begs, "I have renounced all of my wealth, family, and social status to seek enlightenment, and have now even renounced my simple dwelling, but still nothing has happened. What must I do?"

To this the monk simply replies, "You must renounce all you have," and starts to walk on. But this time the man stops him and angrily implores, "But I only have this tunic, a begging bowl, and a copy of the Vedas. I have renounced everything else. If I build a fire and burn these last things, will I find liberation then?" The old man replies, "You must renounce all you have."

Beside himself with grief, the man shrieks, "So must I toss my body onto the fire as well? Then all that will be left are my bones and ashes?"

The monk pauses, looks at the man with that particular mixture of empathy and frustration that is usually evoked by precocious toddlers, and finally responds, "Listen to yourself. You speak of everything as if it were yours to renounce to begin with. You speak of '*my* wealth' and '*my* family' and even 'my bones and ashes.' Even after your supposed death, you speak of these things as if they were still yours. It is this sense of 'my-ness' that you need to renounce. Then you shall find what you are seeking."

Gurevich concluded, "This parable is fascinating to me because it illustrates the different ways we can view paradise (or the afterlife in general). If one believes 'heaven' or 'paradise' is a place where all of our desires are 'fulfilled,' this presents a range of possibilities as to the exact nature of this 'fulfillment.'

"In the Western traditions, we mostly think of this as some version of a twenty-four-hour Vegas buffet. Heaven is a place where we get a mansion and a celestial yacht; where the streets are made of gold and we can eat as much as we want and never get fat. But in the Eastern traditions, the word 'fulfill' is approached from the other perspective. In other words, paradise is not a place where we get everything we want, but rather a 'place' where we no longer want anything. From this perspective, we can see that even nonreligious people can hold a view of the 'afterlife' as a time when they will no longer suffer precisely because they will no longer exist."

He summed up, "The issue of being conscious of this after it happens is another thing altogether. They will exist only in the sense that 'they' will return to the undifferentiated ocean of nonlocal consciousness: as a drop of rain returns to the ocean. Or in the dominant metaphor in Buddhism, their candle's flame will be extinguished for lack of fuel. The burning of desire produces suffering. The way out of this is not, in the Eastern traditions, to hit the metaphysical lottery, with heaven as some sort of eternal game show where we get to pick new appliances and Sandals-style trips across the galaxy from a bedazzled rotating platform. No, the afterlife is exactly that, 'after' life. It is re-absorption into what Joseph Campbell calls 'the Ground of Being.'"

He said there are those who don't believe in an afterlife at all, and some who don't believe in a god but still think there is some kind of nonafterlife afterlife. Gurevich said, as in the parable, "I think the perverse thing has been the attempt to deny (or on the other side overly control, define or manipulate) this seemingly essential part of the human experience, individually and collectively.

"Many rational folks may not take it to the point of making proclamations of faith about one day sitting on a whipped cream cloud and playing harps with Aunt Betty, but something in their reptilian brain nonetheless whispers that they should pack a carry-on bag just in case. After all, not all of us can be pharaohs."

CHAPTER SEVEN

VOICES FROM BEYOND

Everyone has heard stories, or even had near-death experiences, signs from the dead, ghosts, and other signs that the dead are among us. Does this prove the existence of an afterlife? Or are these bits of "evidence" just a product of our overly active imaginations?

Almost everyone has a story or knows a story—you find a penny on the day of a loved one's funeral, and you just know that person is sending you a message. Grandma appears at the end of your bed to tell you she's okay. A feather drops from the sky.

Or even more intense—you've seen a ghost or had a visitor. You hear the voice of someone who died years ago. You go to a psychic and she contacts a member of your family who's passed on, or you're playing with a Ouija board and it spells out something no one alive could possibly know.

Or maybe you think it's all a bunch of hooey.

The 2009 Harris Poll on what people believe found that 42 percent of those polled believe in ghosts, with Christians—at 41 percent—slightly more willing to believe than non-Christians—at 34 percent.

The 2008 Pew Forum survey found that 18 percent of people said they had actually seen a ghost—up from 9 percent in 1990. And the same survey said that 29 percent of people believe they have talked to the dead, up from 17 percent in 1990.

An AARP study has even higher numbers. Among the pool of 1,000 people older than 50 who took their poll, some 53 percent of responders said they believe in spirits or ghosts. And 38 percent said they have felt the presence or seen something they thought might be a spirit or ghost.

In all the polls, women are more likely to believe in ghosts or say they have spoken to the dead than men.

"My sense in studying the history of spiritualism is that people are fascinated with the idea of ghosts because it allows them to give some shape to the uncertainties that arise in the experience they have of their own consciousness," Weber State University Assistant Professor of History Brady Brower told the *Utah Standard Examiner* recently. "All sorts of unexplainable things happen in the lives of normally functioning individuals."

UTAH

While American belief in ghosts hovers around one-third of the population, a Utah psychic medium told the *Standard Examiner* that state has much higher numbers. Kim Terry, whom the newspaper describes as an Ogden-based professional rescue medium and ghost hunter, said that in Utah, belief in ghosts may be as high as 70 percent. Terry said much of that has to do with the heavily religious nature of the state, including its culture (Mormon), and "the expansion of people's spiritual awareness."

"I think they go hand in hand," she said, adding that part of the Mormon Church's ordinances include baptism for the dead. She said church members wouldn't do that if they didn't believe in the hereafter. She told the newspaper that trying to contact God enhances people's belief in ghosts.

Many of our survey respondents, no matter what their afterlife beliefs, were skeptical about contact with the dead. But some said they knew it to be true: it happened to them.

GHOST STORIES

Ashleen O'Gaea said she has had many experiences with visits from, or contact with, the dead. "I had a visit from my grandfather several years after his death, in which he offered the same sort of comfort I got from him when he was alive," she said.

"My other favorite [ghost] encounter was when I was a journalist, interviewing a feature subject. I had my questions listed in my notebook, but when she invited me in, the first thing out of my mouth was, 'It's nice to meet you. Did someone die here recently?' In the recliner in the living room, I could see the impression of someone seated—the Naugahyde appeared indented and outlined by a faint aura which almost had features. And rather than being completely floored by the question, my interview subject said, 'Yes, my dad died in that chair just three days ago.' It turned out he'd been ill for some time, and died peacefully to the sounds and smells of dinner preparation. We chatted about that for a few more minutes and then went on with our interview."

She said she also had the same type of experiences as a child.

"When I was young, a friend and I 'played with' the Ouija board a few times. Once we had quite a long exchange with a spirit who wanted to talk about World War I, and offered details that we didn't know, but were later able to confirm. This was when Charles Schultz's cartoon character Snoopy was a World War I flying ace, and my friend and I were interested enough to have done some research, so we knew a little about the Great War and its battles—but not what the Ouija soldier told us."

She also said she has been to some seers, those who practice a Northern European brand of paganism. "I wouldn't say the dead are among us in the walking-on-the-street sense, but I do believe they're 'in the next room,' and that if we want to or need to, and are respectful, we can be in touch," she concluded. "And whether or not we have psychic or ghostly experiences, our ancestors and other beloved dead are always with us in memory and in their teachings, and so always a part of our lives and of our strength, and of our future."

Catherine Mills, 84, is a Catholic with a strong faith, but the church's teachings against ghosts and the supernatural have done nothing to convince her that ghosts don't exist. This is because she's had many experiences that involve contact with the dead.

"I believe in angels and signs from the dead," she said. "When I have been in trouble and needed help, I believe angels have taken care of me. There is no logical explanation for the strangers who helped to have 'just happened' along. I believe they were angels sent by God. I never saw those strangers again."

She said her father died in 1974. That year she and her husband and two children went on vacation to Maine. Her husband had to return early to their home in Chicago to work, and she had to drive the children back across the country, a distance she had never driven alone.

"I was quite apprehensive about it," she said. "When it was time to leave, as soon as the children and I were in the car, I felt a dome of protection come down over the car. I was very comforted and knew it was my father taking care of us."

She also said when her mother was in a coma and dying and she was sitting beside her hospital bed, a beautiful smile came over her face and her mouth formed "Frank," her husband's name. Catherine had a vision of her father in a golden light at the top of a stairway waiting for her mother and welcoming her to heaven.

"She died the next afternoon," Catherine said. "My sister and I felt her guiding us all through making the arrangements. We chose the same thank-you cards she had chosen when my father died, and chose the same casket vault she had chosen. We found out about these later. On the way to the cemetery the hearse stopped on the road just before going into the cemetery.

I was driving my car just behind the hearse. My sister was beside me. We didn't know why the hearse had stopped, but a white kitten came around the hearse and crossed in front of my car, then stopped beside the road so my sister and I could see and then it vanished from sight. My sister and I looked at each other and smiled, because we knew it was a sign from my mother that she was fine."

POLITICAL DIVIDE

A 2009 Pew Forum study says that more Democrats believe in the supernatural than Republicans. "Conservatives and Republicans report fewer experiences than liberals or Democrats communicating with the dead, seeing ghosts, and consulting fortunetellers or psychics," the Pew study says. Some 21 percent of Democrats responding to the study said they'd seen a ghost, while only 11 percent of Republicans did. The same goes for contacting the dead: 36 percent of Democrats said they've been in touch with someone who's dead, while only 21 percent of Republicans have.

Caren Gittleman, 55, the cat blogger, has had similar experiences.

"My husband and I are very into psychics," she says. "We were told by a psychic that when my dad passed he would visit me in the form of a feather. Whenever I see a feather I say 'Hi, Dad.' For my husband, he was told his mom would visit in the form of a butterfly. On Mother's Day recently we went to visit my husband's mother's grave. I didn't have flowers so I picked dandelions there and laid them on her grave. When we returned to the car the first song we heard was, 'When you go to San Francisco, be sure to wear flowers in your hair,' immediately followed by 'Elusive Butterfly.' Coincidence? I think not."

She added, "Also, there is a squirrel that lives in our yard that reminds me of my dad. My dad adored food and peanut butter. This squirrel will wait till I bring him nuts (other squirrels do not). I am certain he is my dad!"

Father Damian Milliken, the Catholic priest, said he isn't sure about signs from the dead, but he also has a story. About fifteen years ago, he knew a bishop in Baltimore who worked with hardened criminals. The bishop decided he'd look into setting up a séance (a meeting with a psychic or channeler to contact the dead) with the deceased victims of some of the criminals he worked with in an attempt to get them to face up to what they'd done. He went to a psychic, dressed in street clothes, not in clerical clothing.

The psychic told the bishop that someone was watching over him, and the bishop thought the psychic possibly meant his father or mother. But then she asked him if the name Anthony Ashcroft meant anything to him.

Anthony Ashcroft, it turns out, was a mentor to the seminarians when Father Milliken and this bishop were in the seminary. He had died in Africa while there as a missionary in 1964.

"It's disturbing," said Father Milliken. "I don't know what to think about it."

Ian Clark, sportswriter and science fiction/fantasy author, had a ghost experience of the more traditional kind. Not a visit from a lost loved one, but an actual ghost visit.

"I do believe in these things," he said. "I have had minor ghost experiences, especially at the college newspaper office where I spent many late nights. While there—only when alone—I would experience things like the sound of change or keys jingling in someone's pocket when no one was there, computers turning themselves on, footsteps when no one was there and movement out of the corner of my eye."

IT'S ALL PART OF THE PACKAGE

For some of our respondents, contact with the dead is part of their spiritual beliefs.

John Bear Mitchell said, "In our Wabanaki teachings, calling in the dead by use of any means other than by name in ceremony (and not everyone is permitted to do that unless you're a 'trained' spiritual elder) is not permitted. If this was to be done, one might have a bad experience by calling in a 'bad' spirit or even a dark spirit who will try to kill you or those around you."

That said, "We do have ceremonies we use to 'bring in' a past loved-one's spirit for physical or spiritual help in dire times of need. We also do believe that we can communicate with our dead relatives. We can see them—ghosts as you say, when we call them in. Sometimes in the form of a light or a shadow but not in the form we remember them in when they left this world."

Kendra Vaughn Hovey said, "A few years ago when I was ministering the First Church of Wicca, I was very involved with people who worked as mediums, and knew several people who used Ouija boards (including my own children) to contact deceased loved ones, and shared stories of dreams or happenings that were vivid, realistic scenes of a loved one sharing life lessons or warnings for them. In addition, we held an annual Samhain (Halloween) ritual that was specifically meant to help people contact their deceased loved ones and share a night of remembrance with them. It was believed that the spirits of the deceased loved ones shared the evening with us, and so it was a requirement to eat the dinner meal (the Dumb Supper) in silence so we would not scare away the spirits with loud noises.

"It is this time of year that Wiccans/pagans believe that the veil between the physical and the spiritual world is the thinnest, so several deceased spirits travel between the worlds during this time of year."

But she added, "I am not convinced that that this 'proves' there is life after death. I think that the mind is a powerful thing and can conjure up all kinds of things in an effort to comfort us, but, that is not to say that I believe it is untrue either. I simply would have no way of knowing for sure."

Around the time she took the Afterlife Survey, she posted on her blog, "The other night I shared some watermelon and conversation with a pagan friend. He told me that he has been attending a spiritualist church for the past several months. I was happy to hear that he had found a spiritual home but wondered what the fascination was with that church. He explained a typical service to me: prayers . . . announcements, a short metaphysical type sermon emphasizing caring for and loving all people, and then contact with dead spirits to ask for spiritual guidance. Wait a minute! Contacting dead spirits to ask for spiritual guidance? Why contact the dead when you can go right to the source, right to Divine Spirit (God)? He argued that Divine Spirit speaks to all spirits and we can get just as much information and advice for our lives from them as we could from talking to people who are alive.

"I wondered, then, why not seek advice from people who are alive? Actually, as a metaphysician, I believe that we all have access to the all-knowing, Divine Mind, so we don't need to ask any person for guidance—we only need to go to Divine Spirit for our answers. What is the fascination with trying to get answers from dead people? My friend even said that he believed that not every spirit of a dead person is benevolent. So why bother at all if you could be led someplace less spiritual and loving than Divine Spirit could lead you? And I did say to him, 'Well, it sounds like this is what you believe and I certainly will not judge your beliefs, but how do you know for sure that what you believe is true? He didn't have an answer and remained silent.

"The watermelon was delicious."

Arin Murphy-Hiscock, a Wiccan, said, "I do not believe in angels within a Judeo-Christian context. I do believe in spirits beyond the ones who are incarnate who can be perceived or interpreted to be beings such as the traditional Judeo-Christian angels, however; and in the ability of both those spirits who have passed from this incarnation and the people left behind to reach out to one another."

GUARDIAN ANGELS

Many of our survey respondents, as with many thoughts on the afterlife, aren't sure what to think about talking to the dead, but hold out hope it's possible.

"I have not had first-hand experience," said Larry Hausner, the semi-retired CEO from California. "But I do believe that I have a guardian angel."

Poet Billy Collins, who was raised Catholic, said, "On my desk I keep a holy card with a huge glowing angel hovering above a boy and girl who are crossing a raging river on a rickety little bridge. It's one of my favorite images from my Catholic childhood."

Barbara Grandberg, a retired teacher, agreed, "I wouldn't be surprised if this happens."

Hamid Faizid, an adult education teacher, also thinks it's possible. "We can talk to the dead and the spirits understand," he said.

Scott Moulton, the investment services manager, isn't sure what exactly the force out there is, but said, "I believe that science has produced enough evidence to force us to consider that if these experiences are not the spirits of the deceased, then there are other forms of life or energy that we need to consider the possibility that they exist."

Ashleen O'Gaea said, "My short answer is yes. Part of my personal and very specific answer is that I use the word "angel" only in a secular context, as in, 'Some of my best friends are real angels.' The rest of my personal answer is that I think dreams and . . . serendipitous synchronicities, what some people call signs or omens . . . can feel like communication with loved ones who are dead. I can't say they aren't, and I don't feel any need to say they aren't."

WHAT DOES THE CATHOLIC CHURCH SAY ABOUT GUARDIAN ANGELS?

While every Catholic school kid is brought up to believe in a guardian angel, *www.catholiconline.org* tells us that the concept that every soul has a guardian angel has never been defined by the church, so it's not an article of faith. But it is part of the "mind of the church," so it's part of the more general Catholic belief.

The website also points out that belief in guardian angels can be traced back to the pagans, such as Menander and Plutarch, through Neo-Platonists, Babylonians, and Assyrians, right through the Old Testament, where the view of angels is as the "executors of God's wrath" and messengers and servants of God. But in the New Testament guardian angels have a mission to protect those on earth. Catholics learn as children that Saint Jerome is quoted in the Bible as saying, "How great the dignity of the soul, since each one has from his birth an angel commissioned to guard it."

NEAR-DEATH EXPERIENCES

Dr. Jeffrey Long, a radiation oncologist, recently published a book, *Evidence of the Afterlife: The Science of Near-Death*

Experiences. He contends that near-death experiences can prove the existence of an afterlife.

"I have scientifically investigated over 2,000 near-death experience accounts," he told the Afterlife Survey. "I have an online survey which currently has 150 questions. As a result, I am able to study very large numbers of near-death experiences in depth. In researching these experiences I find, among other things, that near-death experiences are highly lucid and organized events that occur while unconscious or clinically dead. The out of body observations are almost always completely accurate. Even those totally blind from birth may have highly visual near-death experiences."

He added, "Typical near-death experiences occur while under general anesthesia (when consciousness of any kind should be absolutely impossible) and also in very young children, aged five and less." He said that when those having a near-death experience encounter people they knew in life, the person encountered is someone who's dead. He said that's different from any other type of altered consciousness experience. "Near-death experiences are strikingly similar around the world, even in non-Western civilizations. Finally, the aftereffects of near-death experiences are a consistent pattern of changes which occur over many years. My major findings regarding the reality of near-death experience have been corroborated by many other researchers."

He said that there are more than twenty different explanations skeptics have for near-death experiences, and the high number is because none of the explanations make sense. "Near-death experiences are absolutely medically inexplicable. This combination of evidence, and other lines of evidence, convinces me that there is an afterlife, a wonderful afterlife, for all of us. Those having near-death experiences are almost uniformly convinced of the reality of their experience. It appears they are correct."

John Griffin, a professor at World University in Ojai, California, also has a book coming out soon about near-death experiences and after-death communications.

He said the existence of such phenomena "is an option that is plausibly open and available."

"[Such experiences] have millions of supporters, including the experiencers themselves as well as respected and even renowned scientists and medical figures."

"All of this information has become increasingly mainstream and widely available. So unless someone is extremely closed-minded and constricted in their thinking, the optimistic possibility is at least there, even if one has not yet become a believer in an afterlife."

Of our survey respondents, many have heard stories about near-death experiences, but few have firsthand knowledge.

Catherine Mills, the retired medical research assistant, said, "My great-nephew Steve was in a coma for seventeen days. After he came out of the coma, he said he had seen and talked with his great-grandmother and great-grandfather (my parents) and his grandfather. They were in a bright, brilliant light and he wanted to join them, but they told him it was not time yet and sent him back to this life."

She added, "It reaffirmed my belief in heaven."

Skeptics from All Walks

Still, it's tough to sell the skeptics on such beliefs, even religious experts. When asked what he thought about ghostly encounters, the Reverend Damian Milliken replied, "I think they're probably a result of medical procedure, or illness."

And Ken Shouler put it this way, "People facing death are hopeful of an afterlife. People with near-death experiences swear by them, even though they prove little or nothing. They act so certain about the interpretations of their experiences that it's quite amusing."

But Rabbi Ilene Schneider said, "An elderly patient of mine had been left a widow many years earlier. She believed she would be reunited with her husband after death. Her one worry: 'He'll coming running up to meet me, and stop short, saying, 'Who is this old lady?'" I assured her that her soul would be the same age as it was when they had last seen each other, and he would recognize her. Do I believe it? No. But the important thing is that she did, and was comforted by my words."

WOULDN'T IT BE NICE . . .

"The honest answer is no, I haven't had [communications from the dead or ghostly] experiences," said Rhonda St. James, the securities compliance manager. "I believe people like to attribute odd coincidences to something more significant or otherworldly, particularly if they derive some comfort from the idea. Let's face it, if you can convince yourself that someone you loved who has passed away may still be close by in spirit, it's very comforting. But I've had no evidence of it or personal experiences with it.

She said if there are such phenomena, "It's staggering to contemplate. And if there's not, that's equally staggering in a very different way. But if the dead are among us, I'm a little honked off that none of them have deemed me worthy to talk to. Maybe nonbelievers are really want-to-believers who are annoyed that the dead don't want to talk to them."

John Reed, the high school teacher, answered the question about whether he believes in ghosts, angels, and communicating with the dead, "Absolutely not."

"What I think has developed into a belief in any kind of afterlife is a desire to have what we've lost, a yearning to go back to a time when we had something we loved," he said. "That's where ghosts and angels come from: they're fictional or symbolic manifestations of that desire. So it works really well in a story as a metaphor, but again, people tend to think the metaphors are real." He said if they were real, "I think that would make my heart ache more.

"However, I do believe that talking to the dead, using them as a focus, and meditating on what that person might have said or done in a situation can be a powerful way of understanding them or one's own life without them. In that way, people do live on, and they can 'talk' so long as we listen to ourselves."

Elizabeth Daniels, the executive assistant/office manager, has a similar point of view. "Like everything else, I do not know if I believe in angels, signs from the dead to the living, or any other kind of communication with loved ones who are dead," she said. "I have had reasons to believe that my dead mother might have wanted me to know that she was with me and that she loves me. But then again, all of these reasons have come from odd and unwarranted things that other people have said to me. I can choose to take that as a crazy person just talking, or I can believe that my mother is reaching out from the afterlife.

"I do not believe in angels as little flying cupids with harps and halos, but I do believe in people who come into our lives and represent only good, and they turn out to be people that we hope we never lose. I believe in signs and certain other uncanny occurrences that we should pay attention to, but they are just that— things we should pay attention to. I do not think they are signs from God or from the dead. These signs are, of course, a possibility. I just don't spend my time looking for them. I have, however, had a few of those freaked-out moments, where I didn't know what to think of what was in front of my face. Signs? Maybe. I'm agnostic, so anything is possible."

NO GHOSTS

Not surprisingly, those who don't believe in an afterlife scoff at the possibility of communication with the dead.

Michael Hawkins, the college biology major, said, "No, there is no evidence for any of these things. Atheists who accept any one of them boggle my mind."

But this point of view isn't held only by those who don't believe in God. Some of the most religious in our survey also dismissed communication with the dead, ghosts, spirits, or angels. "My mother told my wife she would contact her if at all possible. She died in February 2011," said Jim Robidoux, who is a fundamentalist Christian. "She's still waiting to hear something."

The whole concept angers him. "This is an insult to Christ. He told the religious leaders of his time, 'The only sign I will give you is this, I will raise this temple after three days.' He was referring to his body rising from the dead. It's very arrogant for any of us to think we can, by our own will, do the same thing.

"Angels are from God and the devil as well, fallen angels."

CHAPTER EIGHT

DO ALL DOGS (AND CATS AND HAMSTERS . . .) GO TO HEAVEN?

As much as people wonder what happens to humans once they die, they also wonder what happens to Rover and Fluffy. The ancient Egyptians mummified their pet cats and monkeys and put food for them in the tomb so they'd be able to eat in the afterlife. Some modern-day pet owners have their own version of that belief.

There's a whole culture on the Internet set up around the Rainbow Bridge. Never heard of it? It's where your pets go when they die. There's a poem, several poems actually, and websites, message boards, and interactive memorial sites dedicated to it. To some people the Rainbow Bridge is just a comforting thought that helps get them through the loss of a pet. To others, it's an actual place.

Rainbow Bridge or no Rainbow Bridge, 43 percent of Americans believe pets go to heaven, according to a 2006 *Washington Post* poll.

But belief that pets go to heaven didn't start with the Internet and the Rainbow Bridge.

The Ancient Egyptians firmly believed animals had souls and pets were mummified right along with their masters when they died so they could be together in the afterlife. And many other cultures also believe that animals and humans are all part of one big picture.

Father Damian Milliken has lived in Tanzania, in Eastern Africa, since 1960. Among Tanzanian people, "there's a unity of belief of all living things," he said. When they go hunting, they make a reparation because they are going to be taking the life of a living thing, and that life they are taking is an important part of the universe, even though it's only an animal.

POLL: PETS GO TO HEAVEN, EVEN IF HUMANS DON'T

Americans are pretty consistent about whether they believe pets go to heaven. Both a 2001 ABC News/Beliefnet poll and a 2006 *Washington Post* poll, each with about 1,000 respondents, asked whether pets go to heaven. In both polls, 43 percent said yes. In the *Washington Post* poll, 28 percent said no, 22 percent weren't sure, and 7 percent said they didn't believe in heaven, while in the ABC poll, 40 percent said no. In the ABC poll, pet owners (as opposed to all those surveyed) were more apt to believe pets go to heaven: 47 percent said they do and 35 percent who owned pets said no. Of non-pet owners, only 35 percent believe dogs and cats go to heaven, while 48 percent did not believe they go to heaven. In the *Washington Post* poll, when the people who believe in heaven were asked, "Do you think people's pets can go to heaven even if their owners do not?" Yes, said 93 percent; 2 percent said no.

Jack Vinyardi of Kansas City, Missouri, an ordained interfaith chaplain of pets, said in an article in the *Kansas City Star* that he is asked whether pets go to heaven all the time as he comforts people who are about to lose or have lost a pet. He tells these people there is no faith that claims to know unquestionably what happens to animals when they die.

"It is my job to comfort," he told the *Star*. "I believe we each can find answers to divine questions if we look deeply in our own hearts and ask for guidance there."

Paldrom Collins, the former Buddhist nun, said she thinks our bodies are animal bodies inhabited by "the truth of who we are."

"How could something different happen after the life stream ends for a consciousness in a cat body than that which happens to human consciousness?"

And Arin Murphy-Hiscock said many alternative beliefs are grounded in the ancient belief that animals are all part of the same energy that humans are. "This is a very individual interpretation, according to each practitioner of alternative spirituality," she said. "There tends to be a general neo-pagan perception that animals are manifestations of the energy of nature and/or the divine, and therefore their spirits are as sacred as the human spirit is.

"Some believe that the animal's energy returns to the larger aggregate of nature and/or the divine, others believe that the spirits of pets with whom they had a special spiritual bond will also be met again in the Summerland. The ease with which most pagans view reincarnation and the divine character of nature means that there are those who believe very special pets may also reincarnate to accompany the human spirit, to further support and aid in that spirit's quest for wisdom."

Many of the respondents to our survey believe there's also an afterlife for pets, and they put it very simply, but with basically the same theme.

"In my weird version of events, pets join us in our collective fate and return to great collective energy," says Rhonda St. James. "Which is only fair, since they seem much more evolved than most humans."

Ian Clark, the sportswriter and science fiction/fantasy author, said, "I would hope that they are somewhere waiting for us. Seeing deceased pets would also be something I would hope happens in some sort of afterlife." But he added, "Unless they're pissed about how they were treated. I'm sorry if I didn't feed you well, fishy, but I was only three!"

Brian McHugh, the funeral director, also hopes for eternal life for animals. "If heaven is as wonderful a place as I believe it to be, how can there not be beautiful birds singing, cats purring, and hyenas laughing?"

And Anna Rossi, the 75-year-old bookseller, agrees. "I would like to think that if we have an afterlife, so do all the other living creatures."

MODERN-DAY PET HEAVEN: THE RAINBOW BRIDGE

The most enduring modern-day afterlife scenario for pets is the Rainbow Bridge. Spurred by the Internet and evolving from a poem, this view that pets go to an idyllic meadow where they can romp and play in their most healthy, youthful, and perfect form, seems to hit pet owners right where they live.

When asked about the topic, cat enthusiast and writer Franny Syufy responded, "Most pet owners consider their cats and dogs as family members, rather than just pets. Since their normal life spans are so much shorter than ours, most of us will outlive many pets in our lifetime. Just as we would want to envision our human children who die at an early age to be waiting for us in an afterlife, we need to believe in the same sort of place for our pets, to help ease the pain of their loss. The concept of a heavenly place with fields of grass and flowers, butterflies and birds, and a beautiful rainbow leading to a bridge where our beloved friends wait for us is easier to envision than some elusive place with clouds and angels. The author of the 'Rainbow Bridge' poem was brilliant in painting that lovely word picture."

While for many years the poem was listed on Internet sites as "author unknown," Syufy's research uncovered three possible authors:

- Paul C. Dahm, a grief counselor from Oregon who is said to have written the poem in 1981, copyrighted it in 1994, and published it in a book, *The Rainbow Bridge*, in 1998.
- William Britton, a cofounder of Companion Golden Retrievers Rescue in West Jordan, Utah, who wrote a book, *Legend of Rainbow Bridge*, that was published in 1994.
- Wallace Sife, also a professional grief counselor and the head of the Association for Pet Loss and Bereavement, wrote a poem entitled "All Pets Go to Heaven."

Syufy feels that, whoever the poem's author, the creation of it was inevitable. She wrote on *www.about.com* that a music teacher once told the class that "Music *is*. That is, music is out here in the air somewhere, and it only takes a talented composer to snatch it out of the atmosphere and put it on paper . . . so in effect the writing of music is not a creation, but a discovery."

She said that she believes that's also true of the Rainbow Bridge. "It has always been there; it just took an enlightened soul (or three) to discover it."

She said that while the authorship of the poem may never be resolved, "This sweet story will continue to bring peace and comfort to thousands of animal lovers through the ages to come. And one by one, we will some day be reunited with our loved cats and dogs that have gone before."

She told the Afterlife Survey that the Internet explosion of the past couple of decades has made the poem the phenomenon that it is. "The technology of the past several decades has created a world of immediacy. With the Internet, it didn't take long for people to discover the Rainbow Bridge books, and for the concept of Rainbow Bridge to become viral."

And many of the respondents to our survey subscribe to the Rainbow Bridge scenario for pets.

"I like to think that my beautiful and devoted 'soul kitty' Bobo is playing over the Rainbow Bridge," said Caren Gittleman. "I believe that he looks down on me and watches me and protects me. I also believe he is waiting for me. We lived together for 18 years. People say cats are aloof? No. Bobo lived and breathed for me. Even our vet said we had a bond that was unlike any he had ever witnessed between a pet parent and their pet."

April McLeod, 45, who has owned a pet-sitting business since 2005, has had plenty of experience with pet loss, and the concept of the Rainbow Bridge is a comfort to her. "Ever since I launched my pet sitting business, I've lost many of my dear feathered, finned, and furry clients to old age or severe health complications and each loss was more painful than the next, but once I started blogging about my professional pet sitting life, I formed relationships with other animal lovers who eventually lost their pets to the Rainbow Bridge.

"The blogging community taught me that Rainbow Bridge is a beautiful bridge made of a rainbow that they will cross over when pets die. While on the bridge pets will be restored to full health and vitality and will frolic there until they see their owners approaching us from a distance. As we cross over the Bridge to meet our loyal companions there is great joy and laughter because each party has waited for years to be reunited."

She said the concept doesn't necessarily mesh with the fundamentalist Baptist beliefs she was raised with and her concept of heaven and hell, but those who love animals need the idea to help them deal with the loss of a beloved pet.

"While the idea of Rainbow Bridge seems a bit over the top (no pun intended), I choose to believe in it, because even though this place seems fictional, it is one that makes me feel comforted—because, as a pet sitter, pet lover, and pet owner, I need a fairy tale to get me through each horrible loss."

ALL DOGS GO TO HEAVEN . . . OR NOT

The 1989 animated film *All Dogs Go to Heaven* had a plot only an afterlife believer could love. A dog who owns a casino is murdered by a rival and finds himself in heaven, because all dogs go there. But he wants revenge, so he finds a way to get back to Earth. Once there, he finds he needs to prove himself worthy of going back to heaven.

In a more realistic vein, an Errol Morris documentary in 1978, *The Gates of Heaven*, explores the bond between pets and their owners and what happens when a pet dies. This film follows the founders of two pet cemeteries and the people who want to bury their pets. The film is not the Rainbow Bridge or *All Dogs Go to Heaven*—it looks at the world in full, non-talking-animal realism. And ultimately, it says much more about humans and what they believe than it does about their pets.

"You know that Rainbow Bridge tear-jerker that comes around in email every so often?" asked Ashleen O'Gaea. "I think it's like that. I think everything has a soul, and everything returns to the Goddess, and everything learns from its incarnations in its own way. As for pets, I fully expect my ol' crotch-sniffing dog to greet me at whatever passes for the gate to the Summerland, and I expect to be able to hear my long-gone kitties purrin' at me from wherever in that Land of Youth they are."

WISHFUL THINKING

Some of our responders were less inclined to believe in the Rainbow Bridge but still had hope for their pets.

"I believe that animals have souls just like people do," said Kendra Vaughn Hovey. "So I believe they will have the same afterlife that humans do."

Catherine Mills, 84, agreed. "I don't know what happens to pets or where they go after death, but as special pets live on in our memories, perhaps there is a place for them. I would like to think that."

When asked if he believes pets go to heaven, semi-retired CEO Larry Hausner said, "Most certainly."

And Jim Robidoux, the sheet-metal worker, agreed. "Seems like some pets will go to heaven."

Poet Billy Collins has his own take on what happens to pets after they die. "Dogs go to heaven and write poems about their owners," he said. "Cats are driven to the state line and released."

SORRY, SPOT . . .

Not surprisingly, the respondents who don't believe in an afterlife—some of them very devoted pet owners—simply don't believe there is anything beyond life for their pets. And this makes them feel very bad.

"I think they just die the same way I think people do. They stop living," said Elizabeth Daniels, the 26-year-old executive assistant/office manager. She once owned a dog-grooming company. "I think it's very, very sad, and I completely understand the lengthy process of human mourning over an animal. My pets are some of my favorite people, and I don't have many favorite people, so I have a hard time even imagining how I am going to feel when they die. I do not think they go to heaven or hell."

But she added, "Unlike human beings, animals do not have the potential to be evil. They do not do bad things. They do things that humans consider bad by human standards, but still, this would not get them sent to any hell, in my opinion. Unlike many humans, I think animals deserve all the best. If there is an afterlife, I hope animals get the best of it."

John Reed, the 42-year-old high school teacher, agrees. He said the question of what happens to pets after they die is "somehow a much more heart-wrenching question."

"Because I love my pet, and she loves me, but it's a different kind of love. I can have this conversation, but she can't. My being able to discuss it makes it easier to bear. I just hope that when her time comes, she will be comfortable and leave believing—as much as dogs do believe—she had fun and got lots of treats and belly rubs. But when she goes, I know I'll regret every treat and belly rub I didn't give her."

Rabbi Ilene Schneider said that after pets die "they're cremated and buried and memorialized with funny stories."

John Bear Mitchell, citizen of the Penobscot tribe, agrees. "Pets die. It is not as sad as when a human dies. They live short lives and serve a great purpose," he said. "When they die, they fail to exist."

And Hamid Faizid, the adult education teacher, concurred, "Nothing happens to pets. They just die."

Martin Scattergood, the engineer, echoed that thought. When asked what happens to pets when they die, he said simply, "Nothing."

RELIGIOUS LEADERS SAY . . .

An August 21, 2008, *Kansas City Star* article asked various religious and spiritual leaders what they thought about the prospect of an afterlife for pets. Here's what they told the *Star*:

- **Protestant**—Thor Madsen, academic dean at the Midwestern Baptist Theological Seminary, told the newspaper he understood the desire of people to see their pets but there was no biblical grounds they would.

- **Catholic**—The Reverend John Schmeidler of Saint John the Evangelist Catholic Church in Lawrence, Kansas, said that the Catholic Church traditionally teaches that animals don't go to heaven, but when he sees grieving pet owners, he assures them that God wants them to be happy, and if it makes them happy, they will see their pet again.

- **Muslim**—Scholar Abdalla Idris Ali of Kansas City said that the Koran has no direct references to animals in heaven, but in the indirect references, people get everything they want in paradise.

- **Jewish**—Rabbi Scott White of Congregation Ohev Sholom in Prairie Village, Kansas, said that if the truly virtuous get a blessed existence, then that will include pets.

- **American Indian**—Since most American Indians believe all creatures are interconnected, said Gary Langston, a Northern

---

Cherokee, of Kansas City, Missouri, there is definitely an after-life for animals.

- **Hindu/Vedanta**—Anand Bhattacharyya, a member of the Kansas City area's Hindu community, told the *Star* that souls in animals will eventually evolve to the human plane.

CHAPTER NINE

THE CLOSER YOU GET

One would think that as people get closer to death, they start think-ing more about what happens afterwards. It would stand to reason that the older people get, the more the afterlife is on their mind. But this isn't necessarily true.

Is it surprising, or isn't it, that as people age, the less worried they seem to be about an afterlife? At least that's the case for our survey respondents. Yet our younger responders felt the older set *would* be thinking about it.

"My experience suggests yes, they do," said John Reed, 42, the teacher. "When they can hear the clock ticking, they get more conscious of it." As someone who doesn't believe in an afterlife, he added, "I wonder if it will happen to me, after I've written all this about how I don't believe?"

Poet Billy Collins, 70, looks at it this way, "I suppose if one associates old age with the fear of death, [then they think about it more]."

He prefers to look at it as an opportunity for more insight. "But if old age brings an up-tick in wisdom, then older people are in a good position to consider the many possibilities. For example, can you have a heaven without a hell? Some would say yes. Can you have a heaven without a God? Hmmm? Can you have a hell without a heaven? I find that last one a really interesting scenario. At the end of the world, God tells everyone to go to hell. Heaven was a ruse. That's only a little more far-fetched than the Egyptian belief that the rich pharaoh goes to paradise and the rest . . . well, they were too early for hell, but they descended to an unpleasant place."

ELDERS RESPOND

An AARP poll of 1,011 people over the age of 50 came up with these results:

- 73 percent believe in life after death
- 66 percent say their belief in life after death has gotten stronger as they've gotten older
- 20 percent say they are scared of death and what happens to them after they die
- 47 percent of those who believe in heaven believe it is a "state of being"
- 40 percent of those who believe in heaven believe it's an actual place
- 53 percent believe spirits or ghosts exist
- 38 percent say they have felt the presence or have seen something that they think may have been a spirit or ghost
- 86 percent believe in heaven
- 70 percent believe in hell
- 88 percent of those who believe in heaven believe they are going there
- Those who believe they are going to heaven also believe on average that 64 percent of all people will go there

THE OLDER SET

The oldest respondents to our survey were among the most laid-back about what will happen once they're gone.

The Reverend Damian Milliken, 78, responded to the question with a joke. "My sister recently told me she thinks a lot about the hereafter," he said. "She'll go upstairs for something and say, 'now what was I here after?'"

But when pressed, he said he doesn't think much about it. "My thoughts now are more, if I start something, like building a school, I wonder if I'll see it finished," he says. "But I don't think about the time I'll spend in eternity, I think about my time now—how much do I have left in the bank?"

He built a school for girls in Tanzania in the early 1980s that is going strong, and now he's working on a school for boys. "I want to get the boys' school up and running, I want to get a university started." He said when he thinks about getting his projects done, he wonders, "How much time do I have?"

He recently completed a book of his letters from Tanzania home to the United States and is now talking about compiling volume two. "I have a lot to do," he said. "I will just keep on until I don't get up in the morning."

Anna Rossi, 75, the bookseller, said that she thinks the older people get, the less they think about the afterlife. "I think that I thought about the afterlife more when I was young and more religious," she said. "Now, I feel it is possible, but I'm not going to dwell on it. We should try to live the life we have to its fullest. As I get older and see many of my contemporaries pass away, I feel we should make the best of the time we have left—we can't control what comes afterward."

She added, "If there is an afterlife, great. If not, we won't know, will we?"

And Paldrom Collins, 59, said it's natural, as one gets older, to refine beliefs—not so much because of age, but because of experience. "Certainly our feelings about the afterlife are based on what we have been taught, by our religious training, by our investigation into what is real and what is not real. As we mature, generally we become more capable of holding more complex points of view that are possibly contradictory to the logical, rational mind."

FUNNY OLD MEN

Comedian George Burns, who lived to be 100, and got a lot of laughs out of "old" jokes, said of aging and death: *"I don't believe in dying. It's been done. I'm working on a new exit. Besides, I can't die now—I'm booked."*

And Groucho Marx, who lived to be 86, said: *"Age is not a particularly interesting subject. Anyone can get old. All you have to do is live long enough."*

Larry Hausner, 70, the semi-retired CEO and business owner, said as people age, he believes they do think about what comes after a little more and might be more inclined to consider an afterlife. "I think as people get older they tend to 'hedge their bets' a little more," he said.

Catherine Mills, 84, a retired medical research assistant, who always had a firm belief in heaven and an afterlife, said, "I don't know if people believe more in an afterlife as they age, but it gives me comfort to think about loved ones I have lost and am losing now as we age, and believing them to be in heaven."

THE YOUNGER SET

Our younger respondents think it will be natural to think more about it as they get older.

"As people age, more and more of their beliefs are called into question and they realize that our life as we see it can't be all there is," said Brian McHugh, 35. He's young, but as a funeral director he has a unique perspective. "As people lose their parents, spouse, siblings, and sometimes offspring to death, I oftentimes wonder how can they possibly carry on living without a growing belief that they will one day see them again."

He added, "If anyone has any doubt, simply enter any church, temple, or mosque and attend daily services. You might be surprised at the average age of the attendees."

Ian Clark, 37, said, "I think as you get closer to the end it becomes easier. You begin to miss people that have gone before you and realize you yourself will be gone too."

But Elizabeth Daniels, 26, the executive assistant, embraces the "older" perspective. "Perhaps elderly people want to make sure they 'get right with God' before calling it quits on earth, I do not know," she said. "I do not think, however, that belief in religion and an afterlife comes with wisdom. I think that if wisdom had anything to do with it, people would get less religious as they got older; this includes backing away from a belief in an afterlife."

But then she added, "My grandmother and grandfather on my mother's side are devout Pentecostal church-goers. According to them both, they were born into Pentecostal families and raised that way in the church. The older they both grow, the more children they bury, the more their bones and organs fail them, the more religious they become.

OLD AGE FEARS

A 2006 poll by *Parade* magazine and Research!America found that the biggest fear among Americans as they age is losing their mental faculties. Staying healthy is their second biggest concern.

The poll found:

- 96 percent said it is important that we invest in research to prevent, treat, and cure diseases and disabilities that primarily affect older people.
- 84 percent said they believe they can do things to stay healthy as they age
- 83 percent said they are currently taking steps to do so. Of those, 56 percent exercise and 26 percent watch their diet
- 62 percent listed losing mental capacity as they grow old as their greatest fear
- 65 percent expect to see diabetes cured in the next twenty years
- 59 percent expect to see Parkinson's disease cured
- 54 percent expect to see Alzheimer's disease cured
- 52 percent expect to see heart disease cured
- 48 percent expect to see cancer cured
- 47 percent expect to see HIV/AIDS cured
- 37 percent list declining health as their number-one concern
- 23 percent list losing financial independence
- 29 percent listed declining physical ability
- 6 percent list being dependent on others

"And with every hurricane, tornado, tsunami and earthquake that occurs in the various parts of the world, the closer they believe Jesus Christ is to earth and 'calling his children up to Heaven.' The more of their peers they lose to old age, the more they believe the devil is at work amongst us, causing disease and frailty of the bones and heart.

"To them, the afterlife is something more to look forward to than the lives they are living right now on earth. In fact, the last time I saw my grandmother, she said 'if I don't see you again, I'll see you up there' and she pointed to the sky. To me, this is morbid and unrealistic, but to her and her nearby family and church members, it means everything.

"To my grandparents, there is a literal heaven, and it is ruled by a man named God—a human-looking man that you could find walking down the street—and after we all die, they believe we'll go there and immediately continue living life as it is on earth. But up there, it will somehow be special and different. God will be up there, and for them, that's good enough."

Another of our youngest survey responders, Michael Hawkins, 26, the college biology major, said, "People often do tend towards conservatism in their old age, so that may translate to a greater belief in an afterlife."

He said he'd like to see solid statistics on the topic.

"But I bet a lot of people, believers or not, are willing to make a claim here despite not having ample evidence."

LESS SCARY?

In answer to the question "Does the prospect of an afterlife make death less scary?" almost all of our responders said yes. But, as with all afterlife questions, it's simply not that straightforward for many of those who took the survey. For some it is—simply yes.

But for others, issues of religion, philosophical distinctions, and, of course, plain old cynicism colored their answers.

Simply Yes

Some of those who answered the survey simply said yes to this question with no elaboration. Surely, they surmised, the question speaks for itself. One word can say a lot. But some of those who believe the simple yes went a little farther.

Ian Clark, the sportswriter and science fiction/fantasy author, said, "Yes, especially if you think you will receive answers to life's questions when you die."

And Paldrom Collins, the former Buddhist nun said, "Sure." But there's a catch, she said. "Even the belief in an afterlife does not change the body's terror of experiencing death. It only helps us face the terror more openly. I had a good friend who at the moment of death opened her eyes and laughed and said, 'facing death, terrifying.'"

A Question of Faith

Those in the survey who believe in the afterlife on religious or spiritual grounds see this question from a faith point of view.

John Bear Mitchell, the college professor, said that the belief in an afterlife "absolutely" makes the prospect of death less scary.

"It offers us the chance to see our loved ones again. If death is slow, I've heard it said that death is comforting—somewhat a welcome next step. To leave this frail body—this tired and spent body that has served its purpose for the chance to walk, run, and 'dance' again. I think that this makes it far less scary for them."

Catholic funeral director Brian McHugh also said absolutely. "If you believe in life after death, why be scared of leaving this earth? If one has lived a good life, adherent to his beliefs, and succeeded in making the world a better place, the reward in heaven should be great. Just as important, belief in an afterlife allows the dying to feel comfortable leaving family and friends behind because they have a sense of purpose to their lives."

Matt McSorley, the newspaper editor, and a practicing Catholic, did not find the prospect of an afterlife comforting. His response: "Not really, especially if you believe one of the possible destinations in the afterlife is hell."

And Jim Robidoux, the sheet-metal worker, also said the prospect of hell can make the thought of death scary. "For me, as a Christian, I am always afraid I should have lived better. I should be doing more of what God expects, and stop making so many excuses for sins of commission and sins of omission."

But metaphysician Kendra Vaughn Hovey put that thought into perspective. "I think that death is scary because we cannot be one hundred percent sure of our beliefs, but in death I think it is best not to focus on the afterlife as much as in trusting God with our souls. If we truly believe in God—and it doesn't matter what faith we are—then we should trust that He will be with us in death and beyond, whatever that means."

The Philosophical View

For many, particularly those who don't believe in an afterlife or are unsure of their beliefs, the question is a philosophical one. It's not that the afterlife's existence makes it comforting, so much as that believing in it makes people feel more at ease with thoughts of dying.

Anna Rossi, the bookseller, said that the thought of an afterlife might "possibly" make facing death less scary. "But if there isn't one, we will just cease to exist and that will be that."

Michael Hawkins, the biology student, said, "The idea that we never end certainly does make life less frightening. People don't want to lose what they know and who they love; a second life that lasted for eternity would provide for quite a relief, I think."

Engineer Martin Scattergood put it bluntly. He has a friend who recently lost her father, and she and her father both found it a comfort to believe he'd be in "a better place." So the prospect of an afterlife "certainly made death less scary for my friend's father."

But he added his own view: "When I am healthy I am scared about dying. When I was very ill, I wished to die."

John Reed, the high school teacher, said the thought of an afterlife makes death less scary for people who have behaved well here on earth, but maybe not so much for others. "It's much more palatable than oblivion. Good people feel they are getting what they deserve, a reward for their patience. My guess is that truly evil people either fear death because they fear hell—either the fiery one or the memories I believe in—or don't care about dying because they think there's nothing at all. Maybe that's what makes it easier for them to hurt and kill others.

Rabbi Ilene Schneider echoed that thought, "For those who believe they will go to heaven, yes. For those who have regrets and/or unfinished business here that they believe will hinder their entrance into heaven, a belief in an afterlife makes death more scary."

Then others take a cynical view, wondering why those who believe in an afterlife aren't welcoming death. When asked whether an afterlife made death less scary, Ken Shouler replied, "Yes, so they proclaim. But then why do they hold on to life by taking pills, and dealing with various forms of life support? If they really believed in the afterlife, they wouldn't endure all this. Which tells me that they don't believe, but only hope."

And Elizabeth Daniels, who at 26 is still working on her views in light of coming from a devoutly Christian background, said, "I think that the prospect of an afterlife makes death less scary to people who believe. My grandmother on my mother's side is a devout Pentecostal woman. She believes in every Christian notion that there ever was, including the fact that the clouds will one day part, and Jesus will literally descend on air and 'call all of his children to come be with him in heaven.' When my grandmother was being tested for cancer, I sent her my regards and told her that I know she must be so deeply worried and nervous about getting back the results. She told me, 'No. When you're with Jesus, somehow you just don't care. None of this matters. We are in this world, but we are not of this world.'

"Because my grandmother believes that her body is a vessel stuck on this planet, but that her actual being is on its way to a reserved seat next to God in heaven, she is not afraid of death. But to a person like me, she just seems crazy. I think everyone fears death at least a little. Maybe we don't fear the exact moment of no longer existing. We just fear other things, like, 'Will it hurt when I go? Will I die before my partner? Will my children be able to survive? What kind of money and property will I be leaving to the wolves?' I think these are the concerns of the average person. We wonder about our legacies here on earth after we are gone. Devout people claim not to care at all. I find that unrealistic—and phony."

Mark Henderson, 53, who is in hospice care for his terminal cancer and knows his days are numbered, does not believe there is an afterlife, and said, "I am not afraid to die. I'm concerned about the mechanism of death when it comes. I hope it will be painless. I hope that [life] slips away. I'm concerned about my family; I'm concerned life goes on well for them.

"But what comes beyond the eternal void is just that and that makes whatever moment I have here all the more important."

CHAPTER TEN

AFTER DEATH, WE *DO* PART

Most families have differences in opinion. Some debates are small—whether to roll up the toothpaste tube or just squeeze from the middle. But some are biggies—what happens when we die, how we deal with end-of-life issues, or religious differences in light of that. What happens in marriages and families where beliefs in the afterlife differ?

With the growing divergence in people's beliefs about an afterlife, you'd suspect you'd find giant rifts in families where members have differing views. For example, people who come from a religious background but have changed their afterlife beliefs might clash with relatives who still believe in heaven and hell. Or people who don't believe in an afterlife might not understand the need for ritual or arrangements of family members who do believe.

But surprisingly, among our survey respondents, there are few arguments—mostly because few are talking about it.

However, those survey respondents who deal on a daily basis with families who are facing life-and-death issues tell a different story.

ABOUT MOM'S FUNERAL

Funeral director Brian McHugh, a practicing Catholic who believes in an afterlife, said that in his own family, "so far, we all have the same afterlife beliefs." But he doesn't always see that in his job.

"It is common to work with families where such agreements are not present," he said. "It makes for very stressful and difficult funeral preparations. As society changes, we see more and more younger people not holding the same beliefs regarding death and the afterlife as their parents or grandparents held. They don't see the value in religious rites, life celebrations, and proper burial or cremation."

THE CREMATION ISSUE

Cremation is one of those topics, particularly in religious families, that can cause arguments in end-of-life planning. While some religions specifically prohibit it, Judaism most notably, because of the belief that the soul will meet up with the physical body again when the messiah comes, there is no Christian biblical reference prohibiting it, and most Christian religions allow it.

According to *www.cremationsolutions.com*, the large majority of religions permit cremation. Those opposed include the Greek Orthodox Church and Conservative and Orthodox Jews. The Catholic Church was once opposed, but now allows it, and the website reports that not only have Catholic cremations increased quite a bit over the last twenty years, but the church also allows the cremation urn to be displayed on the altar.

Brian feels it not just as a business issue, but personally. "This is frightening to me as it has been famously noted by a philosopher, whose name I can't recall, that one can compute with near mathematical certainty the righteousness and justice present in a society simply by examining the way that society cares for its dead."

Rabbi Ilene Schneider said that as a grief counselor, she also sees family rifts over differences in beliefs. "In terms of afterlife beliefs, I find that non-Jews often do share common views with family members, but the area in which there is conflict within Jewish families is the subject of cremation. Traditionally, Jews do not cremate, because of the belief that all souls will be reunited with their physical bodies and be resurrected with the messiah arrives. For those who do not share that theology, I explain the Jewish resistance to cremation in terms of the Holocaust, when Jews were burned as if they were trash.

"The major conflict here is when the children or spouse want to honor their loved one's wishes, but those wishes conflict with their own value systems."

Not surprisingly, those with alternative beliefs see more conflict among families over end-of-life issues.

Kendra Vaughn Hovey said when she was a Wiccan, she saw families fall apart because of differing beliefs. "It's sad, but true. Yes, I think how we view God is how we view the world. If God is viewed as a controlling and punishing entity, then that is exactly the way we are going to treat our family members with differing beliefs.

"In contrast, if God is viewed as an all-loving and all-embracing entity, then that is how we will treat our family members with differing beliefs. It would stand to reason that all aspects of life would follow suit based on these beliefs. For example, a devout Christian Scientist would be appalled if you even suggested medical treatment for a terminally ill patient and would have a difficult time accepting a family member who opted for the treatment.

"Death plans, funeral plans, and so many other things are just complications for those who are set in their ways and unwilling to tolerate another person's religious views. Personally, I think it is not enough to tolerate others' religious views, lest we have pity on them for not knowing what is 'right.' It goes beyond tolerance to sheer acceptance of that person. He has made a choice for himself that all we need to do is look beyond religion and love him the way God does.

"But, of course, I believe in an all-loving and all-embracing God."

Ashleen O'Gaea, who practices Wicca, has a poignant take on the topic, seeing with her experience of her parents' deaths how different beliefs can help people come to a new understanding about each other. She said her parents agreed on how to plan for death and their funerals—but their beliefs diverged widely from her Wiccan beliefs.

"I couldn't help noticing that they were both fearful and angry as long as I knew them, which was for over forty years," she says. "I think my dad believed that misfortune in this life paralleled and presaged what would happen in the hereafter, and I know that the preacher at his cousin's funeral preached fire, brimstone, and damnation unto us all. I think Dad thought that we needed to be prepared in this life for that misery, and Mom worried that he was right. I don't think he took any pleasure in it, but I think he thought it was best to anticipate extreme bullying after death."

While her parents' attitude toward death troubled her, the last "conversation" she had with her father as he was dying gave her some comfort.

She said he spelled the word "student" for her.

Ashleen replied, "Perfect, Bobby. Exactly right. You're a good student, good job."

She added, "I know that school in my dad's youth was a violently punishing experience, with hitting and humiliation— bullying—taken for granted, even approved and encouraged. It was telling that for him, the foyer to the afterlife was a classroom. I hope I sent him off to recess with a clear conscience.

And I still thank him for reminding me that we are all students to the end, and beyond, and gain in our new beginnings."

She said she was present for both of her parents' deaths—her mother died ten months before her father—and, "I reassured my parents in the ways I heard them asking to be reassured. I think we all at least hint at our concerns sometime when we're dying.

"What can be hard for family members is to stay open enough, through the personal grief, to take those hints. Sometimes it's hard to move beyond our own sense of loss —not just the physical presence, but of the emotional support we will miss, or have always missed—to meet with someone else's needs when they did not meet ours, and our own remain unmet.

"I had some issues with my father, yes. But my instinct was to give him the care he needed, so that I could later reinterpret my memories of his approach to caretaking."

She added that she wishes her parents could have seen their lives, the legacy they left, and what happened after as a more positive thing. An incident at her father's funeral helped bring this thought home to her. A friend who came to support her ended up speaking spontaneously at the ceremony. He was a veteran who had never met her father.

"It seems my dad's work to repeal a double tax on veterans' benefits had resulted in quite a number of vets getting unexpected refund checks, some for sizable amounts. And at the service, this man who'd never met my dad thanked him for the windfall."

"To me, that symbolized an attitude, a trust, that I wish my parents could have embraced. They focused on duty, on staying out of trouble or getting what was due them by virtue of their following the rules, without ever understanding that everything we do affects others, and what others do affects us, and that's not always a bad thing. When we open ourselves to the process, it's a windfall for all of us.

"That fundamental perception, which I learned from my practice of Wicca, affected how I said goodbye to both of them, but not at a particularly conscious level. Now, thinking out it in relation to various memories I have of Dad and Mom, it affects they way they are still present in my life, the way I think about my own mortality, and the way I counsel others who are facing changes in their lives."

> ### BEYOND CREMATION—DISSOLVING
>
> The latest way to dispose of a body after a person dies goes way beyond cremation. Alkaline hydrolysis, which uses heat and lye to turn the body into a liquid that can then literally be washed down a drain, is catching on among many who believe it is cheaper and more environmentally friendly than burial or cremation. The dry bone residue that is left over is given to loved ones to do with as they please.
>
> The method, also known as resomation, dates back to ancient times, but until recently it was only used to dispose of cadavers at medical schools and for animal carcasses. It is legal in several states, but only one funeral home, in Ohio, actually practices resomation.

"There are a few things I'm not ready to talk to my dad about yet—but I still thank him for reminding me that we are all students, to the end and beyond, and again in our new beginnings."

WHAT DO YOU MEAN, WE WON'T MEET UP?

In the case of Martin Scattergood, the 53-year-old engineer, the topic hadn't come up between himself and his wife until he took our survey, even though he suffered a nearly fatal illness with a long, precarious recovery.

He said after he took the survey, "My wife and I were on a journey for a weekend away. I told her about the questions and how I didn't believe in an afterlife. She was unhappy about this because I wouldn't be looking over her when I die."

When he asked her to elaborate, she told him she was convinced he would die before her and she was disappointed he didn't believe in the afterlife.

"I asked her to explain what she meant by her comment, 'You will not be looking over me when you die,' because I told her that if she believes in the afterlife I will be there and I will do it. Her answer was both revealing and thought provoking. She replied 'it will be more comfortable for me if I knew you believed you would be looking down on me.'"

Franny Syufy, an About.com writer, found herself in the same position as Martin's wife when her husband died in May 2008. "For various reasons he had lost his faith and believed that we just cease to exist when we die."

She said that has made her interested in any information about the afterlife she can find. "I'm trying to keep a grip on my own faith because that seems like such a harsh end to life, and at seventy-four, I need something to hold on to."

Don't Ask, Don't Tell

Martin and Franny's experiences are atypical of most of our survey respondents. The majority say they've never even discussed the topic with family.

"We haven't had to plan these things," said Anna Rossi, 75, of end-of-life decisions. The topic of afterlife beliefs simply hasn't come up in that context in her family. But noting that she has six children with varying beliefs, she said, "I'm sure there will be disagreements."

John Reed, 42, who doesn't believe in an afterlife, has made a point *not* to discuss the topic with his family. "I don't—and won't—tell my family about my beliefs," he said. "It would grieve them too much. I'll go along with the prevailing belief. It doesn't hurt me at all to do it, and would make their lives worse if I don't."

"We haven't discussed it," said Barbara Grandberg, 60. "But my mom probably thinks she'll be joining my dad."

Arin Murphy-Hiscock, a pagan and practicing Wiccan, said that those with alternative beliefs can face challenges when it comes to end-of-life decisions. "I see a lot of friction between individuals and their families when it comes to planning any rite of passage, such as marriages or funerals," she said. "Concerning death planning, it's imperative that any practitioner of an alternate spirituality write out his or her wishes in their will, so that religious beliefs and preferred practices are respected. Expecting the family to plan and handle a ceremony of a religion not their own can be awkward, so naming a specific person or group of people from the individual's spiritual community to handle the spiritual ceremony is a thoughtful thing to do."

She added that, "Often there is a disconnect between the individual's family and the spiritual community, and so two separate ceremonies may be performed."

She said that in the case of two ceremonies, often the family's ceremony concentrates on the body, while the spiritual community would have a private ceremony "sometimes using the individual's spiritual tools or specific possessions to represent their connection to his or her energy and life."

Caren Gittleman, like many of our survey responders, really didn't have an answer to the question about whether differing beliefs would cause a family issue. And it was the most common answer we got. "Frankly," she said. "We never discuss it."

ONE BIG HAPPY FAMILY

Most of our respondents were confident that there wouldn't be any problem—while they haven't discussed it, they know their family members feel the same way they do or are at least comfortable with each other's beliefs.

"My father and I have different beliefs on just about everything, and that does affect our relationship," said Matt McSorley, the newspaper editor. "But afterlife isn't a significant issue there. As far as [end-of-life planning and medical decisions], the people whose decisions I would be involved in have the same outlook I do."

Brian McHugh, the funeral director, said he sees the difference with families who are all in agreement. "In the funeral business, it is common to perform funeral services for multiple generations of the same family, and it is astounding the composure, love, respect, and dignity surrounding the deaths in families that have a strong belief in the afterlife."

Semi-retired CEO Larry Hausner said his family members all have different beliefs, "from nonbelievers to born-again Christians."

"It will not alter my plans to be cremated," he said.

Catherine Mills, 84, the retired medical research assistant, believes in heaven, and added, "I don't believe my family has different beliefs." But she said, "If you love a family member, then you try to do what [he or she] would want. I think your love and respect for the person should govern any actions and their wishes should be considered."

John Bear Mitchell, 43, of the Penobscot tribe, said his beliefs allow room for other beliefs and that family differences don't matter. "I have family who have decided to take the religious route in the their lives—Catholics and Protestants. They respect my beliefs and are very interested in what I know and are happy to share their beliefs, too. Sometimes they ask about combining the Native American with their beliefs or they search for the parallels. The differences do not affect our relationships."

He said when it comes to end-of-life decisions, "As for funeral planning or medical decisions, whatever the beliefs of the deceased may be dictates how we honor their bodies."

Elizabeth Daniels, 26, the executive assistant, is another one who hasn't discussed her beliefs with her family—she doesn't believe there's an afterlife, but comes from a firmly Christian background. Some family members, she's pretty sure, would be affected by her beliefs. But her immediate family—father and siblings—knows how she feels and it doesn't seem to matter.

"My family members all believe differently, but so far, it has not affected any relationships. When I am with my Pentecostal grandmother, I keep mouth shut and my head down, and I attend church when she tells me to. I sit there wondering how the whole crowd of people can be in the mindset that they're in, and I feel sorry for them, but that is all. I have not told my grandmother that I am not a Christian, because that would be the last day that she would ever speak to me if I did. My father's wife is a religious woman. She believes in angels and heaven and hell and that any great thing is somehow divine intervention. She also believes that the Bible is the word of God and that every ounce of it is true, so of course she believes in the afterlife. My siblings all claim to be Christian and do not know even the meaning of Easter, but they believe in the afterlife. They believe in heaven and hell, as does my father."

She added, "Everyone in my immediate family (father, siblings, stepmom) knows that I am not Christian, nor am I religious in any other form. None of them care, however. They are fine with what I believe, because I do not try to convince them [to abandon] what they believe.

"I think that everyone could be fine with everyone's opinions if humans stopped forcing these things on others so much and making such a big public deal of how they choose to worship. Relationships are affected and wars are started when people all start arguing about what 'the truth' is, as if anyone has the right answer to this question. No one does."

Michael Hawkins, 26, an atheist who doesn't believe in an afterlife, said the issue of different beliefs so far hasn't caused any family conflict as far as end of life decisions go. "Most of my family holds some sort of religious belief or at least think there is a god," he said. "Interestingly, religious discussions never dominated my family, so there really has never been any conflict."

And Ian Clark, the sportswriter and science fiction/fantasy writer, said, "I'm not aware of too many of my family members' thoughts on the afterlife, though I don't think they would be far from my own, since my family is not religious."

Dealing with It

Mark Henderson, a former minister, is facing his end-of-life decisions right now. Mark is in at-home hospice care as he deals with terminal cancer. In practical terms, he is doing "legacy work." Not only is it focusing on getting everything together for a memorial service, "but how you deal with looking back and what kind of legacy you want to leave behind," he said.

And his humanist views and belief there is no afterlife are actually making the process easier—for him and his family.

Many people outside of Mark's family believe that since he was a Christian minister, he believes what ministers believe, and he goes along with it. He says, "It doesn't come up because people make their own assumptions."

His wife, to whom he'd been married for just a year at the time of this survey, and his 17-year-old son share his afterlife beliefs. In

fact, his wife is very conscious of the fact that her father's humanist beliefs—including having a military atheist symbol put on his
gravestone, which he was adamant about—were ignored by family making the decisions after his death. And it bothers her.

Mark recently told his son that even though he doesn't believe
that he would have a connection with family after he died, "It
would be nice to think there would be some kind of connection in
a general cosmic sense." And his son replied, "What? Why would
you want there to be?"

"I thought that was interesting," Mark said.

While he understands how that "cosmic connection" or even
the traditional Christian idea of your loved ones watching over
you, influencing the universe on your behalf, "would be lovely
to look forward to," he said he feels dwelling on what he knows
won't exist simply takes energy away from focusing on the here
and now.

He and his wife have talked about what it's been like for couples who have been together for a short period of time, like they
have, having that feeling "that they will always be together, eternity that will always bind you . . . and we are so closely connected
and have been right from the start, so there is this sense of, How
could this end? How could this possibly end?"

But he's realistic. "Part of what we're facing bluntly is that her
life will go on without me, and I'll be gone. And that's that. I've
been asking myself if that adds much of a burden, and I haven't
felt it."

He added, "What it does now is it compels me to be as alive
as I can for all these people I love. It makes my time here more
precious, because I just can't just slough it off and say 'I'll take
care of that in the afterlife.' If I have time to do it now, I will do
it. Some of it is practical, making sure they have what they need,
and some of it is making sure that when we have time together,

we take advantage of that time. It makes this time more precious. And that's okay."

His parents were "typical liberal Christians" when he was growing up, and he hasn't discussed his afterlife beliefs with them.

"I don't know what my folks think. We haven't really talked about it," he said. "I think they see [my cancer] as a really shitty draw as well, and they're horribly sad because of that, but I don't think there's going to be any big issue and I don't feel compelled to kind of clarify it with them. They seem to be okay with the things I'm talking about and things I'm not talking about. We're not sitting around saying, 'Let's pray.'"

Many people in a situation like his would be ending phone calls with, "I'll pray for you."

But he said, "Our phone calls end with, 'I love you,' and that's pretty cool."

CHAPTER ELEVEN
THE LIGHT AT THE END OF THE TUNNEL

When people are touched by tragedy or experience wild success, it often has an impact on how they see the world, and it also affects their afterlife beliefs. Some people's beliefs evolve as they experience life's bigger ups and downs. For others, beliefs are clarified. Surviving a near-death experience, being in a profession that deals with death every day, or facing a terminal illness can all clarify what a person thinks will happen after death.

Most people, through the religion they've been exposed to, the reading they've done, and the conversations they've had, have thought at least a bit about heaven and hell or what will happen when they die.

But some people have thought about it a lot more.

For people whose lives have been tough . . . who've experienced tragedy and heartache . . . who've dealt with death in their jobs, these thoughts are more real. It's an obvious concept—nothing makes people think about an afterlife more than an unhappy existence here on earth or the concept of death itself.

Yet some people just believe there's got to be something better because it's too hard to believe there *won't* be something better.

And for almost everyone, once it's close (for you or someone you know), it's hard not to wonder what's going to happen.

Brian McHugh, the funeral director, has seen every variation on afterlife views. "My role in the funeral industry has only solidified the teachings I received as a child," said the practicing Catholic. "The old saying 'there are no atheists in a fox hole' is remarkably accurate. When people are faced with the prospect of imminent death, they often search for some belief to soothe not only their frightened body, but more importantly, their quivering souls. They may take the time to prearrange their own funeral arrangements, if for no other reason than to lessen the burden for family members.

"However, they also search for answers as to why this is happening from the world around them, and not surprisingly, they find nothing. No infomercial, sporting event, or even close human relation can soothe the anxiety surrounding their own death. Can this really be the end? This is where the prospect of an afterlife resonates most loudly."

He added, "People who are expecting an afterlife, in whatever form they believe, are more relaxed and accepting of a terminal diagnosis. Their families are in turn more comforted as they expect to see their loved one again, but next time, in a more glorious state."

John Bear Mitchell said that his life experiences have contributed to his belief in the afterlife.

"I feel that this has all evolved to give me peace of mind and hope for those times when it feels hopeless. I have lost a child to suicide and have had a child taken from me without cause. My belief in the afterlife has helped me develop peace in times of great grief and loss and has helped my other two children walk with their heads up and gives them the freedom to ask questions of the spiritual strength I have developed. This spiritual strength has (inadvertently) been a role model for my two remaining children."

Dr. Jeffrey Long, the oncologist, has documented many near-death experiences. He has a unique view on people and their afterlife beliefs. "I am a radiation oncology physician, which is the use of radiation to treat cancer. Nearly all of my patients are facing a life-threatening illness, and many are beyond hope of cure. I am impressed at the variety of attitudes that patients have toward their illness. Most of them show great courage," he said. "The patient's belief in an afterlife, and their families' belief in an afterlife seem to be very important in facing life-threatening illness. This certainly seems to improve their quality of life."

HAWKING'S FAIRY TALE HAS NO HAPPY ENDING

Physicist Stephen Hawking has motor neuron disease, an offshoot of amyotrophic lateral sclerosis, which is often called Lou Gehrig's disease, a progressively paralyzing terminal illness. Hawking has lived with the prospect of death for forty-nine years, he told the English newspaper the *Guardian*, "I'm not afraid of death, but I'm in no hurry to die. I have so much I want to do first. I regard the brain as a computer which will stop working when its components fail. There is no heaven or afterlife for broken-down computers, that is a fairy story for people afraid of the dark." (See Chapter 12 for more of Hawking's beliefs.)

And Paldrom Collins, the counselor and former Buddhist nun, believes what people go through in life has a big impact on how they view what happens after.

"Being present when someone dies can have a radical impact. Facing death, being diagnosed with a terminal illness, or surviving an incident in which death is faced head-on can change feelings about this life and thus the afterlife. We are also impacted by others—studying, reading, and hearing from those who have greater wisdom coupled with [our own] internal investigation, experience, and maturity can certainly alter our views."

But Rhonda St. James, the securities compliance manager, who has dealt with tragedies in her life, said, "They did not necessarily affect my view of the afterlife, but rather showed me that bad things happen to good people and good things happen to bad people."

WHAT'S LIFE GOT TO DO WITH IT? (THREE STORIES)

The afterlife is something that's been a big part of the lives of some of our survey responders. Either through dealing with family or through personal experience, they've had cause to seriously consider what they believe and what it means to their lives.

Elizabeth's Story

Elizabeth Daniels, who in Chapter 9 discussed one set of grandparents' fears as they get older, sees a big divide in how the older generations in her family view death and the afterlife versus the younger view—much of it forged by hard times, ingrained belief, and family tragedy.

Elizabeth's grandparents on her mother's side are white and Pentecostal.

"My great-grandmother and my grandmother on my father's side (who are black) are Baptist. They are as devout as my Pentecostal family members, but in a different way. That entire [Baptist] side of the family is very involved in the church, and they will not so much as eat a Jolly Rancher without praying over it first. My great-grandmother was alive when African American people were supposed to sit at the back of the bus and drink from 'colored-only' water fountains. In those days, African American people were being hosed against brick walls by police, and to hear my great-grandmother tell it, all of those police are now burning in hell for what they did.

"During my great-grandmother's younger years, black people barely had a voice in society. All they had was each other, God, and prayer—hope, really, if you ask me. I read somewhere once that religion is a thing born of fear. On both sides of my family, white and black, the elders are absolutely the most religious. They are devout and fearful of God and a living devil. They talk of a rapture and a New Jerusalem. They believe in these things with everything they have, because it really *just might be* all they have, and they likely don't know how to think differently anyway—even if they wanted to. Belief in God was the only kind of real hope they ever had. They come from a time when things in this country were a lot worse off than they are today, believe it or not, as far as civility goes.

"My Pentecostal grandmother has buried one child after a suicide (my mother) and another after a homicide of a gunshot to the back of the head when she was sixteen years old. She lost another to muscular dystrophy. Today, her only other two living children don't have much to do with her—only on holidays, they'll come around. One of them is 'well-to-do' in the CIA, and the other lives in New Mexico and has AIDS. Neither of them believe in an afterlife, so far as I know. In fact, they keep a distance from my grandmother because of her strict ways, mostly to be blamed on her religion and the fact that she disagrees with today's generation entirely. My great-grandmother on my father's side (who is black) had one daughter, who began having children at the age of fifteen. Of her three children, one became a felon, the other still lives with my grandmother and has a number of children of her own, and the other's my father.

"It seems to me that as the times change and the rate of college graduates increase, the amount of extremely devout religious people decreases to a small extent. In my grandparents' day, the idea of an afterlife was easily accepted and passed down. There was no reason to doubt that there was a heaven, a hell, God, and a devil. The elders of the white side of my family did not like black people, and the elders of the black side of my family were afraid of and consequently hateful towards white people. By the time I came to be, all of the elders were upset. Both my mother and father were told on different occasions that they were going to be sent to hell because I was conceived. Even at that time, the strong belief in an afterlife was prevalent with my elders—even if it was being used as a form of punishment. It was everything. It was watered down with my mother and father, and with me—it's barely present at all. But the people of my generation are also more free to wonder and decide things for ourselves, I think. Tradition becomes less and less important these days, and doubt seems to be increasing in popularity. It's all about independence and freedom of this and that—we think about things before we accept them. We wonder how fairy tales have been so easily bought into by the masses of the past, and continually passed down as a result of such gullible and unquestioning belief. Some people today are more focused on saving the environment than praying for their souls.

"My grandparents however, do not waver in their beliefs in Christ. They just feel more and more sorry for the people of today, who are surely going to go to hell when it all comes to an end. And this 'end' grows more and more near every time it quakes in California or rains in Seattle. My grandparents believe that they are 'in this world, not of this world.'

"I think that they probably carry that belief from a time where they had to think that way as a method of survival. The people before them probably believed it too, because being 'of this world' was a very scary prospect when you were either persecuted or put on a pedestal due to the color of your skin.

"I hate to admit it, but the way my grandparents think makes a lot of sense to me. I don't like it, and I don't agree with it, but I understand it. And as they feel sorry for me, I feel a little more sorry for them."

Martin's Story

Martin Scattergood is an engineer who owns an international company. As a scientist, he doesn't believe in an afterlife. A nearly fatal illness that kept him in the hospital for sixteen weeks didn't change his mind.

"In 2005, I was extremely ill. I stopped breathing and unbeknown to me, I was only seconds away from death. I did not have any conscious thoughts about any afterlife or anything beyond my physical world.

"I was put into a medically induced coma. I'd suffered total paralysis, was on life support, in severe pain and unable to communicate. When I awoke from the coma, my quality of life was extremely poor. On two occasions, I thought about wanting to die. I wanted to escape from my new horrible world. As far as I was concerned at that time, death was also total finality. But my condition was so bad that I considered it a much better option than continuing to live.

"I have reflected on both of these experiences. The first one was terrifying as I fought against the illness that was attacking me. I really believed I was going to die but after stopping breathing I blacked out and was not aware for several weeks how close to death I had been. When I found out, I was terrified and it remains a very strong fear of mine that I will contract the illness for a second time, driving me towards death again. The conclusion I must draw from this is that I am afraid of dying.

"The second experience contradicts my statement above. When I was experiencing very poor quality of life, I was seeking death as a way out, as an end to my suffering. Putting both experiences together, I must conclude that feelings about death have to be taken in the context of the present quality of life.

"Finally, I was discussing the death of a friends' father last month. My friend was at his father's bedside in the final hours of his life. They both took comfort from their deep religious beliefs and believed as death approached that he was going to a better place."

He said that the friend he was discussing the death with made it clear he "believed in an afterlife and that such a place was much better than our living life—i.e., it is a 'better place.'"

"I respected her beliefs, but was unable to comprehend the thought of an afterlife until I reflected on her words a 'better place.'"

And his own experience gave him cause to examine the concept. "I reflected deeply on my experiences after waking up from the coma and had to conclude that although I did not believe in any afterlife, I had to agree that when my quality of life was so poor, death was really a 'better place.'

"Perhaps the afterlife is then really only a matter of definition and is dependent on the quality of one's life?" He points out that dying made his friend's father fervently believe he was going there and helped ease his fears. And he believes his quality of life colors his view on how he feels about death, even though it doesn't change the fact he doesn't believe there's an afterlife. "When I am healthy I am scared about dying. When I was very ill, I wished to die."

Mark's Story

Mark Henderson, 53, became a Methodist minister at the age of eighteen. He officiated his first funeral on his nineteenth birthday. He got a master's degree in divinity from Boston University and became a church pastor and a hospital chaplain.

And somewhere while all that was going on, he got married, had a son, got a divorce. And got cancer. Beat cancer. Got remarried. And his cancer came back.

At the time of this survey he was in hospice care, told by doctors there was nothing left that could be done. But he was feeling pretty good, considering, managing his pain and his symptoms at home.

But, said Mark, "I know realistically once you get to this point with pancreatic cancer, it can move on you—[it] can be like I am right now and then things go to the liver and go downhill fairly quickly."

Somewhere along the way, through thinking about religion, what he had learned, and what he saw through his own experiences in life, Mark became an atheist. And that hasn't changed with his illness.

In talking about his family and the possibility of "looking down on them" or having some connection from an afterlife, he says "it would be lovely to have that connection to look forward to. But even though I would want that, I can't even feel compelled to get to that point, to believe it just because I want it," he said.

"I could take all those comforting images and comforting words that I have shared with others, and claim for my own, but I feel no need to do that." He added, "It's not a negative thing, it's just not a part of what I sense or feel."

Faced with imminent death, he said, "What it does now is it compels me to be as alive as I can for all these people I love." And atheism is actually a help to him.

"There is no level at which I believe this happened because of a plan or a reason," he said. "This is a random unlucky draw from the deck and makes it easier for me to deal with it." He said he wished more people recognized the randomness of this type of thing, because then maybe it would spur them to learn more about pancreatic cancer and other illnesses that hit people out of the blue and kill them.

He acknowledges that his point of view may be hard for some people to deal with. "They've been told if you don't believe in an afterlife, somehow you're out of whack and life isn't right."

Growing up he "had your generic liberal Christian belief, there is a god who loves us.

"I had a sense there was a loving god and when we die we become part of that oneness, that wonderful community of saints. In the end, hopefully, if we don't have our understanding too messed up, you'll meet Grandma, you'll meet Grandpa [in heaven]."

When he officiated his first funeral, "I didn't even know the person. It was your standard little homily about how we go along in life, and sometimes we're taken out too early, and we're taken down stream by our father who guides the boat and takes us home . . . ."

He said that by the end of his active work in the church, he would occasionally identify himself as a Christian humanist in the pulpit, and for a while had "this new age-ish belief in an energy, a force, that when we die, we go back into that river.

"That's nice fairy tale stuff, it's fun to read *The Hobbit* and it's fun to read *Star Wars*—fantasy is fun to read, but that was wrapping up my fantasy world as it related to theology."

He said when he finally let go of the fantasy world, "It was such a freeing thing. All of a sudden now, this life was as precious as it seemed. Almost like everything in life was kind of turned up a notch or two. Everything seemed kind of beautiful and horrific to me, because everything was real and our relationship to it drives the meaning.

"I feel quite content that we derive meaning from how we relate to the absolutism of what we see around us. The nonsupernatural reality of life. We've got life before us and what we do with it is what life means to us. It's pretty engaging and for me it's more than enough."

He said hardcore Christian beliefs like fundamentalism and Pentecostalism "seems to me to be drawn out of an unreality—they're so harsh and people don't want to deal with [the realities]."

He cites Harold S. Kushner's book *When Bad Things Happen to Good People,* which has been popular for decades. "Here's a guy who went through various things in the Jewish scripture. And all it said was, 'Why do bad things happen to good people? Because they do. You enjoy life, live life to its fullest, and sometimes this happens.'"

He said people are moving in that direction, "But they live in churches that build big buildings and want them to be biggest thing on the block and don't want them to think. They've got products to sell. When people start thinking for themselves, they find out they don't need all that.

"In fact life is more engaging when you let go of all that crap and start thinking for yourself. Evolution for me is that you never stop asking."

He said he was always exposed to death. "I chose to confront the question of death all my life."

"I got to this point, well, and here is where I stand."

He said several years ago he watched the movie *The Truman Show.* The movie ended with the main character's rejecting the fantasy world that had been created for him and walking out into the unknown.

"I was really pissed off by it. It disturbed me so much because I was not yet ready to walk through the door. I was at the door, but I wanted to go back to the island, be back in my secure life. I didn't want to face it.

ENJOY EVERY SANDWICH

Few celebrities have had the final days of their lives scrutinized the way singer Warren Zevon did after he was told his lung cancer was terminal. His final record album, *The Wind*, took on the topic with humor, grace, and poignancy, particularly a rollicking rendition of Bob Dylan's "Knocking on Heaven's Door" in which at one point he sings, "Open up, open up."

He scoffed at those who said he was a hero for refusing treatment after he was told it would only prolong his life briefly, and he said his message was the same as it always was. "To me, the message of my songs, of all songs, is '*enjoy* life.' My message as a person who evidently doesn't have much more *planned* is the same. It's the only message I ever *thought* art had any *business* having."

In 1993, a decade before his death, he told *Entertainment Weekly*, "If you're *lucky*, people like something you do early and something you do just before you drop *dead*. That's as many pats on the back as you should *expect*."

Shortly before his death, he appeared on the *Late Show with David Letterman*. When David Letterman asked him if his experience gave him special knowledge, Zevon famously said, "I know how much you are supposed to enjoy every sandwich."

"For me change was getting to point where I walk through that door. I love the fact that there was no light on other side of the door [in the movie], that he walked through into darkness."

He added, "What I had found on the other side of the door was a whole world I hoped would exist and be more beautiful than anything I could imagine."

And then he got cancer. "Now bring it to bear with this bullshit. I don't sit around blaming god, being resentful of god, being resentful of life, blaming life. I feel I can deal with things in a more straightforward manner because there's nobody to blame. What's happened has happened and I don't have a belief set that drags me down to use my energy in ways that are counterproductive."

"I feel that through and through, and makes it easier in some sense. Keep going day to day. What can I accomplish today? I won't be able to accomplish much for too many days, but what can I do today?"

"It's visceral in that a lot of the bullshit in life sort of fades away. We all have our prejudices and things. I'm really less concerned with a lot of the banality of life. Right now, things seem much more simple, much clearer. What I need seems clearer, what's going on in the world seems clearer. I feel compelled in the midst of that to feel authentic and live with as much integrity as I can. It's simple—be who I can be. I'm empowered by the need to be as honest as I possibly can so when the moment comes, I can leave behind that level of honesty. People won't wonder what they meant—we will have shared that."

To any suggestions that he's taking a high road many in his situation wouldn't, he said, "No, make no mistake. This isn't noble. I'm not just sitting around being noble. One thing this is not is noble. I have made mistakes in my life, I've made mistakes in judgment. There's times in my life that I've hurt people because of my mistakes in judgment. I'm compelled to look at everything, look at the overall sense of my life. Is there anything I owe anybody? Is there anything I owe myself?"

He concluded, "I feel at peace with that. There are people who will not have kind thoughts about me when they hear I've died." But that doesn't bother him. "I need to make sure I've done the work I need to do, precisely because it matters. I can't rely on that glorious day where god claps me on the back and all is forgiven. When I die, that's the end of it.

"I'm making sure the work is done, and taking seriously the life I have left, and dealing with it the best I possibly can."

Mark died July 24, 2011.

CHAPTER TWELVE

SCIENCE: FOR OR AGAINST THE AFTERLIFE?

Two forces that have always been at loggerheads are science and religion. Is belief in an afterlife trumped by scientific belief? How do the two things fit together? Our survey responders mull over whether there's any room for science and an afterlife to abide peacefully.

For many people, the idea that an afterlife could be explained scientifically is impossible. The two things are diametrically opposed. Both people who practice a religion and those who live by scientific belief are pretty adamant about it.

And there have been a host of scientists—most famously Albert Einstein and Stephen Hawking—who are atheists because the belief in an afterlife cannot be supported by science.

But what if it could? Some of the respondents to our survey think maybe that's a possibility.

In fact, a recent book by an oncologist, *Evidence of the Afterlife,* purports to scientifically prove there is one. Jeffrey Long, who treats cancer patients and has documented more than 2,000 near-death experiences, says his research tells him that science and belief of an afterlife aren't incompatible at all.

"Through my work and the work of others, I believe that scientific methods can be used to study evidence pointing to an afterlife," he said. "When I first started out, I would not have believed this. It took a mammoth amount of evidence, and corroboration with other researchers' findings, to come to this conclusion. At the current time I believe that experiences like near-death experience are extremely important for research, and yet have strikingly little funding sources available to allow such research. I hope this changes the future."

He added that he believes that lack of funding for research is in part caused by the reluctance of many to mix science and faith.

"I think the lack of funding for near-death-experience research is due to several causes," he said. "Probably first, it is so non 'mainstream' that there are just no research funds designated for near-death-experience research. Second, due to the lack of research funds, it is difficult or impossible to get academic researchers interested in doing this type of research."

He thinks it's likely the scientific community's skepticism is the root cause.

In a 2010 interview with *Time* magazine, he elaborated that his research addresses what religions have been saying all along, that there's an afterlife, and therefore order and purpose to the universe, and a reason for us to be here. He said that the only aspect to human existence that science can't touch is what happens after death—after that, it's all about faith.

YES

Long tells the Afterlife Survey that his research has confirmed what he believed all along—and made his belief stronger.

"I was probably like most people growing up in the state of Iowa," he said. "We belonged to a mainstream Protestant church. I accepted the reality of God and an afterlife on faith, but was always uncomfortable with the concept of faith, given that I was raised in a very science-oriented family. (But) I now believe that strong evidence regarding the afterlife is available from scientific study of certain phenomena."

Though they didn't do the type of research Long did, many of our survey respondents agree that there may be a way to scientifically prove the afterlife—but with a strong dose of faith thrown in.

John Bear Mitchell said, "I feel like a lot of scientists are looking at the possibility but they are looking in the wrong place—Earth. I don't think there is proof in that respect."

And Paldrom Collins, the former Buddhist nun, agreed, "Science is just another way for people to explore the unknown. If it helps people prove or disprove something, or be more comfortable within themselves concerning their beliefs, then it's valuable to them. I do not consider science antithetical to spirituality."

Scott Moulton, the investment services manager, said he's not sure. But "I believe science has begun to provide enough evidence to show that 'paranormal' phenomena does exist—whether it's spirits caught in the afterlife or some other form of life force we cannot consistently measure. There is something there."

Ian Clark, the sportswriter and science fiction/fantasy writer, has the same view as Scott.

"Truly scientific? No. But things like disembodied voices that can be recorded and things of that nature and my own experiences are enough for me to believe in ghosts."

Kendra Vaughn Hovey also thinks the two may go together. "I do not see science and religion as independent of one another," she said. "I guess it just comes down to tracing things back to the point where we no longer have the answers, and there we will find God—the unexplained. No matter how much we know about science and how many things we can discover there are always questions that cannot be answered. God simply made it that way."

Rabbi Ilene Schneider said she can see it either way—that people allow what they believe to determine their view of reality.

"They are two different systems. Science needs proof. Religious belief—faith—only exists in the absence of proof. Can they co-exist? Humans have a remarkable ability to hold two conflicting views simultaneously."

NO AFTERLIFE

John Reed, the high school teacher, believes advances in science continue to provide evidence that there is no afterlife—although it hasn't gone all the way yet. "Proof? No. Strong suggestions? Yes," he said. "As the universe is understood, better and better, I think the mysteries we have attributed to deities in the past will become less mysterious.

"It was my understanding of the Olympic gods that led me here: when people had no science, they thought everything was caused by gods. The more they understood, the fewer gods they needed. Now, most people believe in one God, so whenever something they can't explain happens, they say he did it. But as we unravel the clues around the mechanisms of those mysteries, we'll have, as a society, less need for belief in that area. But I doubt we'll ever really figure out death, so there will always be a belief in an afterlife."

John joins a host of scientists who have publicly said they don't believe in an afterlife, most recently Stephen Hawking.

When the physicist author of *A Brief History of Time* told England's *Guardian* in May 2011 that "there is no heaven," and that the afterlife "is a fairy story for people afraid of the dark," it caused an uproar.

Hawking's 1988 book famously said that if scientists could develop a "theory of everything" then mankind would "know the mind of God." But in his 2010 book *The Grand Design*, he says that the existence of the universe can be explained without the need for a creator.

In the newspaper interview, he said in answer to the question "Why are we here?" that "The universe is governed by science. But science tells us we can't solve the equations, directly in the abstract." In addition, "Science predicts that many different kinds of universe will be spontaneously created out of nothing, It is a matter of chance which we are in."

SCIENTISTS TALK ABOUT GOD

A few months after Stephen Hawking told the *Guardian* that heaven is a fairy story, the newspaper sat him down with another physicist, Brian Cox, to talk again about science and God. This is part of what the two had to say:

When Hawking said that science can be explained "without the need for a creator," Cox called his answer "beautiful" and said that "knowing the mind of God" actually was the same shorthand Einstein used to "convey the majesty and beauty of the laws of physics, and did not intend this to be taken as a sign that he subscribed to a particular religious doctrine." Hawking agreed that's what he meant, but since it's not what most people mean when they refer to God, he decided to stop using the term.

The scientists in our survey agree.

Michael Hawkins, the college biology student, said, "There are positive reasons to reject the idea of any intervening god: the laws of the universe act indifferently to humans, prayer does not work, life evolved, natural selection is necessarily blind, chance events really are chance."

He added, "Any idea of an afterlife that requires a god of this sort has evidence against it. But there could be some other sort of afterlife, or god could be hands-off and we just got really lucky, and so the lack of evidence is my primary appeal. The burden of proof is always on the believer."

HAWKING BACKLASH

Stephen Hawking's comments about heaven not existing got a severe backlash from Christian bloggers. For instance, Rob Kerby, a senior editor on beliefnet.com, points out that some of Hawking's scientific conclusions have been questioned by other scientists, and that Hawking's first wife said his "scorn for religion" is one of the reasons their marriage broke up.

"So, Hawking has now taken up theology—although he has no credentials on the subject, but instead biases so deep that they undermined his marriage."

"So there is no heaven? Well . . . maybe not for you, Stephen." Ouch.

And that was one of the more civil attacks on Hawking. Why the vitriol in an age when science is prominent and a scientist's disbelief in a traditional heaven should be par for the course?

We asked E. Brooks Holifield, the Emory University professor. He cited the Pew Forum survey results showing belief in an afterlife, and said, "The point of Christianity has always been salvation . . . . The majority think that they will exist eternally in a heavenly realm, regardless of how they define it."

And apparently, they don't want a scientist telling them otherwise.

Martin Scattergood, the engineer, who also doesn't believe in an afterlife, said belief in science and an eternity after we die just don't go together. "I am an engineer, I see things logically and I can not find any evidence or proof that would point to an afterlife. I also can not see any scientific or even nonmetaphysical way that an afterlife could exist. I do not believe in an afterlife and I am sure that there is no scientific evidence to disprove my belief."

Elizabeth Daniels, the executive assistant/office manager, isn't a scientist, but has considered the topic. "I feel like scientific proof more supports a disbelief in the afterlife than it does a belief in the afterlife. This is due to the obvious: no afterlife or otherwise religious idea or popular belief has ever been scientifically proven."

She added, "I'm a huge believer and supporter of science, by the way."

IT DOESN'T MATTER

Those in our survey who practice a religion faithfully are less invested in the question because they believe the answers come from God.

Larry Hausner, semi-retired CEO, said science plays a part "only to a certain extent, because I think God allows 'alterations [in belief].'"

And Jim Robidoux, the sheet-metal worker, takes exception to the "fairy story" characterization.

"People from the time Christ died to the present time are not only dying, but are willing to die for Christ. I do not believe the biblical stories are fairy tales, they are the truth. Christ's disciples would not be willing to die for a pack of lies. They were beaten, tortured, imprisoned, exiled, crucified, stoned to death, thrown out of the synagogues and through the centuries even now are dying because of their faith.

"God makes himself known and he won't be denied."

Brian McHugh, the funeral director and practicing Catholic said, "I feel there is no scientific proof to either support or refute my belief in an afterlife."

And Matt McSorley, also a practicing Catholic, said firmly no, there is no scientific proof to support his belief. "And there can't be. Science deals with what is observable on Earth."

CHAPTER THIRTEEN

THIS IS YOUR BRAIN ON THE AFTERLIFE

In the end, humans need to define why we're here. What's it all about? The need to know hard-wires humans to believe in an afterlife, most of our responders agree.

Since human life began, the prospect of an afterlife has been a matter of debate, hope, despair, consternation, and big ideas. Nowhere is that more evident than in our survey respondents' opinions.

The one question that looms almost as big as "What is an afterlife?" or "Is there an afterlife?" is the most meaningful question of all: "Why?" Why is it important for many—or most—people to believe there is something beyond what we've got here?

The majority of our respondents said it comes down to comfort.

"Yes. It gives meaning to life," said Rabbi Ilene Schneider. "It answers the question 'If this is all there is, why bother?' It gives hope and comfort."

Hamid Faizid put it more simply: "It gives people hope."

And Ken Shouler put it even more succinctly. It's human nature, he said, "because people are scared of dying."

IT'S ALL ABOUT FAITH

Respondents with a religious view of an afterlife believe there is more to this answer than simple human relief at not being totally gone.

Jim Robidoux, 52, the sheet-metal worker and devout Christian, said it's not so much human nature but a matter of faith, and those who believe, the way he does, believe because of faith, and not because of any human emotion or need. "I believe what the Bible teaches," he said. "We will all be raised, some to eternal life, some to judgment that will be horrifying."

He added, "Anyone who seeks after God with his whole heart will find him."

Brian McHugh, the funeral director and practicing Catholic, said that before technological evolution, it was human nature to believe in an afterlife, just because no other explanation for what happened on earth was evident. "Humans need answers to difficult questions, like the meaning of life."

He said the tide has turned, and the more scientific discoveries made, the more answers we have. But we still can't answer the big one—whether there's an afterlife or not. So humans have to pick at it. "It's human nature to question the afterlife," he said.

Catherine Mills, the retired research assistant, responded, "Yes, I believe that humans need to believe in God and heaven. If they didn't [believe], if this life were the only thing and there was no god or heaven, I think there would be chaos and that humans would be very greedy and selfish."

And according to Kendra Vaughn Hovey, "The answer is simple—it is truth. Humans know truth when they see and hear it."

IT'S A MATTER OF NEED

Billy Collins, the former poet laureate, had this take, "Sure, it's understandable that we would construct pictures of the unknown, and we can easily understand how some would use these scenes to control behavior given our appetite for power. It's also very human to gamble, to make a bet, as Pascal suggested, with 'le pari.' That is, behave as if there were a God and a heaven. This does not even require belief. Just buy into it. If you're wrong, no loss. If you happen to be right: eternal salvation! Good odds."

Many of our afterlife responders, whether religious or not, shared that view.

For instance, Brian McHugh said, "The simplest way to for me to think about the possibility of an afterlife can be summarized by this sentence: I would much rather live my life on earth believing there is an afterlife and find out there isn't one, than die and find out there is one!"

But Rhonda St. James, the securities compliance manager, said, "I think ego has more to do with it than human nature. Oh wait, ego *is* human nature. Okay, no hairsplitting. I believe that our egos tells us that we are so unique, so very, very special, that of course we cannot just cease to exist. All the wonderfulness that makes us who we are couldn't possibly just go nowhere. Could it? So yes, it is human nature to want to believe that our unique individual self must continue to go on in all of its fabulousness."

"But I don't believe it," she added.

Elizabeth Daniels, the executive assistant/office manager said, "I think it is human nature to want and need to be comforted and pretend we understand everything, just for the sake of saying it. I guess this includes a belief in the afterlife. It feels better to think that we can close our eyes and talk to a loved one who passed on, rather than to accept that they perished and disappeared like a tree that has been cut down from the forest and taken away."

Arin Murphy-Hiscock, the Wiccan priestess, agreed. "I think the sense that awareness or some part of our energy continuing on is a comfort for many people. The not knowing, the uncertainty, or the thought that things just stop is somewhat antithetical to the natural idea of movement within life and energy, so the prospect of the forward-moving energy continuing in a different form/place is definitely a comfort."

Larry Hausner, the semi-retired CEO, sees it as more than comfort to people. "I think that most people feel somewhat inadequate about themselves, maybe due to the trials of everyday living, and this alone would give credence to wanting to believe that there must be a better place after we die."

AND WE'RE MADE THIS WAY

Whether it's a matter of religion or just the need for comfort and an explanation of the unexplainable, many of our responders believe that humans were made to believe that something comes after.

John Reed, the high school English teacher, said it's a little counterintuitive. "Oddly [we are hard-wired to think this way], because we can reason. I don't think animals think that far into the future. But we can. So even though I think it was my capacity for reason that led me to my beliefs [that there is no afterlife], I think that same capacity also leads to the apparently logical [or at least hoped for] conclusion that there's more after this."

Paldrom Collins, the former Buddhist nun and counselor, agreed. "In being present at birth and death it has been my experience that a portal opens. Some still, loving expanse is present. For me it doesn't seem possible to live through those moments without a belief in some existence other than the existence that we normally experience as 'being alive.'"

So did Matt McSorley, the newspaper editor. "From a human standpoint, the idea that existence just ends is probably hard to wrap our minds around."

John Bear Mitchell, the college professor, said, "I do believe that it's human nature to believe in the afterlife and I also believe that if someone is not going to believe in an afterlife, then they spend more time convincing others that they are correct than they do convincing themselves that the afterlife does not exist."

Michael Hawkins, the biology student, looked at it this way. "Humans are able to perceive and assess causality at a greater level than any other animal. That provides for a framework where misattributions can be made and faith can flourish. Further, religion is a cultural phenomenon that plays directly into the fact we are social animals. Its very nature may not be inevitable, but it seems very likely. After all, what human society has not had religion?"

He added, "There are a number of reasons people want to know what happens when we die. Some people are purely curious. Others are interested in intellectual questions. But I think most people are afraid. It is often said that people become atheists to avoid the judgment of God, but it seems impossible to me to claim that avoiding such judgment is better than annihilation. The end of my existence is a disconcerting concept, but any fear that may have driven me to ponder the question cannot force me to conclude anything else."

Ashleen O'Gaea also said humans are wired to believe in something more. "Because our experience in our three dimensions (okay, four if you count time) is that there's always something after. In primal societies, it's not just a belief that the ancestors continue to participate, it's a behavior. Cycles and continuities are among the first things we humans recognized in the world, and I do think that's part of our nature."

And Anna Rossi, the bookseller, said, "I think religions evolved because the universe is so vast and mysterious that people had to believe in something to explain it and keep order, e.g., the ten commandments."

Mark Henderson has a master's in divinity and was a minister for most of his adult life. He said people are definitely hard-wired to believe in something bigger. "We know that we are hard-wired to tell stories and create patterns," he said. For instance he said, when man first evolved, "And there are two of them out in the wilderness and they hear the grass rustle. One of them knows it's a lion and he's the one who will probably live." So we began to tell stories—"Not in some nefarious way, but that helped us to survive. So you would know who to trust, and make sense of a world that's big and dangerous. Make a path to survival.

"So why would we end that survival because our bodies don't last? We see some plants go away, and boom, they come back the next year. So why wouldn't we continue to extend that survival?"

The storytelling "helps us know our lives make sense." He continued, "And as society becomes complicated, the more we need that. Rulers of Egypt were bound and determined they were part of everything, they were not mortal, they were going to connect themselves to the cosmos. And if you've got the pharaoh who's connected to everything, and we're connected to the pharaoh, then we're connected to everything, too."

Mark said he saw a play about Galileo in which the great scientist couldn't understand why a student wouldn't back him up. And the student said something like, "You're asking me to say to my parents that their life is not the center of God's universe, so their suffering is not at the center of God's plan. If this earth goes around a sun, who knows where God is? I will not take that hope away."

He added, "It's a poignant moment. Dramatic. And it's a metaphor for the way a lot of people deal with this stuff."

He believes people also need to know their lives will be redeemed, that everything makes cosmic sense. "The ultimate argument is people say, 'Are you going to tell me someone like Hitler just dies?' People don't want to hear it . . . . People have shame ground into them by the church, this is its wonderful hook, you need some way of recognizing punishment is real, because if there isn't any punishment, what does it say about the nature of your own crimes? You need the images to keep you in line. 'There but for the grace of God' is a very real concept."

SO DOES BELIEVING MAKE PEOPLE BEHAVE?

Andrew Gurevich, professor of literature and philosophy at Mount Hood Community College, said it's easy to tie belief in an afterlife and human behavior into religion, but that's not the whole story.

"Religious traditions all present their followers with some view of the hereafter. In most cases the emphasis is on instructing the hearers on how to act and make moral choices in their present lives (think 'Ghost of Christmas Future'). Cosmology (the study of origins) helps us understand how we got the way we are. Eschatology (the study of the end times) helps us figure out how to 'fix' it. When we can look at our lives, our present choices, from the perspective of their future consequences, we can make appropriate choices to help influence the more desirable outcomes.

"So for many, even those who may not actually believe in a real heaven or hell, the vague notion of the afterlife helps them navigate their current moral climate. Think of it as karma. Think of it as what you would like to be said at your funeral. Think of it as protecting your brand." He added, "In any case, I am suggesting here that there are many people, religious or not, who look at the present from the perspective of the future. I am not sure this qualifies them as 'believers in the afterlife,' but it may count for something in the discussion."

And he contended that, "This exercise works wherever you start the clock. In other words, if you want to understand yourself in your present state, try thinking back to your childhood and the significant choices you made (or more likely were made for you) and how those choices led to more choices, which in turn helped shape the person you are today."

And our responders believe that afterlife beliefs do have some impact on people's behavior, but not wholly. They had different conclusions about it.

"I think that, again, most people are basically good, and would not alter their way of thinking," said Larry Hausner. "However, with that being said, I do feel that a lot of the excessive evil of our times is created by people who do not believe in an afterlife."

But Anna Rossi said, "I believe that we should live a good life no matter what. Many people who believe in an afterlife are the cause of much suffering in this world."

And Ian Clark, the sportswriter and science fiction/fantasy writer, said that he feels that belief in an afterlife definitely makes a difference for many people in how they behave during their life. "The very religious seem to be consumed with it to the point of thinking of nothing else except where it will lead them at the end."

Almost all of our respondents said that no matter what they believe about an afterlife, they try to be good on this earth because of this life.

Clark's response was typical of many or our survey takers. "I don't think [what will or won't happen in the afterlife or] believing in an afterlife has an impact on me. My core beliefs are based more on what it is to be a 'good person' than what it means for me down the line."

The more religious people in our survey agreed but also looked toward what they believe comes after.

"'Love the Lord your God with all your heart, with all your mind, with all your soul,' and 'Love your neighbor as yourself' seems a small price to pay, even if there was no afterlife at all," said Jim Robidoux, the sheet-metal worker. "Your benefits in this life will be incomprehensible, the afterlife is just more gravy, and more cherries on top."

But those who don't believe in an afterlife also made a case for themselves.

Martin Scattergood, the engineer who survived a bout with Guillain-Barre syndrome, a disease that paralyzed him and put him in the hospital for sixteen weeks, felt being ill makes him behave differently, but not because he's afraid of where he'll go when he dies. "I try and live my life differently because of my illness and near-death experiences. As far as I am concerned, the afterlife is irrelevant because it does not exist. What does exist is the enjoyment of being alive. If we are healthy and have family and friends, we are incredibly rich and so very lucky to be alive."

HELL? NO!

One of the biggest findings of the Pew Forum survey was that people's beliefs had changed a lot from what they were raised in, and almost half of those polled didn't believe in hell.

Our survey found that to be true, too. Even many of those in our survey who still follow an organized religion shy away from the version of hell that they were taught as a child.

Ken Shouler said the rejection of hell should lead to the rejection of an afterlife as well. "Carl Sagan was fond of saying that the comfort value of a belief does not increase its truth value. Amen. But people need a thumb to suck on, and the afterlife provides it. You can almost hear them saying, 'Hell? Ooooh! I can't believe in that terrible place.' Fine. So why then believe in the afterlife?"

Andrew Gurevich said the change in people's beliefs goes hand in hand with the way our modern culture operates. "A famous Russian playwright once noted, 'Advertising is the very essence of democracy.' Religions now market themselves to a consumer culture. We are used to it, and actually expect it. We want to be courted and flattered; focused-grouped and exit-polled. There are 137 different kinds of pasta sauce, designed for every kind of taste preference. Why not at least as many kinds of afterlife? You like your heaven extra cheesy, I like mine with chunky garden vegetables. That guy over there is into a paradise of pesto. My mother is partial to an afterlife of Alfredo."

He added that these days hell seems to be reserved for "the designated 'out' group *du jour*: homosexuals, feminists, atheists, liberals, Darwinists, terrorists, or the more amorphous secularists might go to that 'other place,' but we good folks who comprise the 'in' group already have our tickets to the ball.

"This tendency to flatter people into the pews (and keep them there), when coupled with the increasingly taboo subject of teaching religious ideas in the public schools, has created a nation of people who are guided by these religious memes as filtered through our materialistic consumer culture. And like with other products, we are allowed, even encouraged, to church-shop in the same way we shop for HD TVs. We are consumers of heaven now. And the customer is always right, right?"

But most of those in our survey see it differently.

Why do people abandon the traditional idea of hell?

One of our respondents tells why she went from believing in hell to not.

April's Story

April McLeod is a pet sitter who was raised in a strict fundamentalist Christian home.

"As a child reared in a strict Baptist home I was taught that Jesus loved me so much that he died on the cross to pay for my sins . . . and that he would meet me in heaven when I died. At the tender age of five I was unclear who Jesus was, especially since I only saw him in storybooks, but my parents seemed to like him, so it was only natural for me to accept him into my heart just as soon as I could learn to recite the Sinner's Prayer. I really didn't understand the words of that prayer, but I did understand that if I didn't recite the words that I was bound for hell." She said the picture of hell painted for her was one where "sinners would scream and cry out for water while burning in a lake of fire."

But as she got older, "I could not understand why God would punish nonbelievers so severely in hell. To me, God represented love, and as the years went on I started to doubt that he could be so cruel to those who chose not to follow his path to the letter.

"To this day, my parents are independent fundamental Baptist Christians who taught me to believe that the only ones who will go to heaven are those who accept Jesus Christ into their hearts. In addition, anyone who consciously behaves as a non-Christian will go to hell." She said being a good person or a bad person makes no difference, in her parents' eyes.

"I did believe what I was taught about the afterlife because I did not know any other beliefs about the afterlife existed. A child who questioned her parents' words was a child who was rebellious and a shame to the family, so therefore I never dreamed of questioning anything my parents said until years later.

"After attending various independent fundamental Baptist churches I began to realize that church, for me, was a place where judgment of others was paramount, and since I believed that God was not a God of judgment, but of love, I grew to despise organized religion. It was more about impressing other people and showing your face in church rather than nurturing a relationship with God."

She said when she made mistakes in life, her church family wasn't there for her. "The judgment that was placed upon me for my sins nearly convinced me that God had the same feelings of judgment toward me, and as a result of those beliefs I was certain I was going to hell when I died.

"Once I stopped going to church I began the healing process, and during that time I was reminded of what God is really like: a God who forgives and a God who wants everyone to live with him in the afterlife."

Now she says, "I do not believe God wants to make it difficult for anyone to get into heaven, because I believe God is a God of love and not of judgment."

CHAPTER FOURTEEN
IT'S ALL GOOD

While our survey respondents can debate the afterlife and what it does or doesn't mean until they find out for themselves, most of them believe that if there is an afterlife, it's open to almost everyone of any faith. And more importantly, it's life here on earth that counts the most.

It stands to reason that if someone believes there is life after death, he'll say his view is optimistic. And most of our responders who believe in an afterlife say they do have an optimistic view.

As Brian McHugh, the funeral director, put it, "Why not be optimistic about the possibility of an afterlife? Why would anyone want to believe our whole existence ends in a slow ride in a hearse?"

What may surprise some is that those who don't believe in an afterlife also believe their view is optimistic. For example, John Reed, the high school teacher who doesn't believe there's an afterlife but does believe we live on in the memories of others, said, "If I didn't think I could influence others to do good and to help society, I wouldn't strive so much to be remembered as an ethical person. I believe that my attempts, even though they are on a small group of students, will make the world a better place."

And there it is in a nutshell. How our responders feel about an afterlife is actually tied up in life itself. You can't get away from it. And it's the view of life here on earth that colors the view of what may come after.

"A BETTER PLACE?"

The phrase "a better place" is often used to describe the afterlife. Many people count on the idea that they'll go to a better place; they not only count on it, they look forward to it. And they're happy to feel that way. Even those who don't have a specific religious belief and aren't sure what awaits say believing makes them feel good.

But others who believe say it's not necessarily something to feel good or bad about; it just is.

The Believers

Ian Clark, the sportswriter and science fiction/fantasy writer, said, "I think I am optimistic about it, yes. I'd like to be able to see old family and friends and pets or visit in some way, to watch my children or grandchildren or even great-grandchildren at key moments in their lives."

John Bear Mitchell, the college professor, said he's optimistic about the afterlife, "But at the same time, I'm optimistic about next week, too."

Some of those who believe in an afterlife have a darker view.

Jim Robidoux, the sheet-metal worker, said, "I am truly afraid more people will die not knowing God than will know him. I know Christians who think God will save so many. It will be a great surprise. I am hoping God does great miracles with mankind."

And Kendra Vaughn Hovey said, "I think people are generally scared and confused and try not to think about death and the afterlife until it is staring them right in the face. I think that if we focused more on our relationship with God, perhaps through very regular prayer and meditation, we would get a glimpse into what life with God would be like after the physical. Once we can grab hold of that Truth there is nothing to fear and only peace in the knowing. May we all have peace in the knowing."

Catherine Mills said, "I believe my beliefs about God and heaven are optimistic. I don't feel God created people just to send them to hell."

And Rabbi Ilene Schneider said, "In my experience, even though a few (very few) have been frightened because they believe they will be going to hell, most believe they will be in some sort of heaven."

Not Knowing Is Okay

Those who are less certain of an afterlife still think their view is optimistic. Since they can't know, they work on life here on earth. Bookseller Anna Rossi said, "I don't believe anyone will 'burn' in hell. If there is an afterlife it will be the same for all, and we will understand the mysteries of the universe. If there isn't, it really won't matter."

And Arin Murphy-Hiscock believes most people are optimistic in their views: "I feel that generally, people want to look forward to something positive, either as a comfort for a hard life, or as validation for a life well lived."

Ashleen O'Gaea said, "I hope [there's an afterlife], and I would like it to be so, but I see such fear behind so much behavior [by people who believe in one] that I wonder sometimes. On the other hand, I do believe, as I've probably written in more than one book, that we can help each other through our fears, and come to a love that will bring us optimism in our beliefs about each other, ourselves, our gods—about our lives, our deaths, and our afterlives and next lives."

The Bright Side of No Afterlife

Elizabeth Daniels, the corporate executive assistant, said that she thinks believing in no afterlife at all is more optimistic. "I think that my belief on what happens to humans after death is very optimistic. I think that an afterlife actually lacks optimism, because it is basically the belief that a person lives on forever, even if their soul takes on another body. And I think that is unfair. If there is an afterlife, I personally hope that I get to start over with another brain. I have too many negative memories in this life to carry on with me any further after my present body dies. It would only be torture to have an afterlife, even if I was a bug sitting on a leaf, reflecting on what my life used to be. Might I miss my past life as who I am now? Or might I sit around regretting that life if I was still unable to get over the things that hurt me?"

> **WALK LIKE AN EGYPTIAN**
>
> A book, the Egyptian *Book of the Dead*, was found next to mummies in ancient tombs, and its hieroglyphics were finally deciphered by Champollion in 1824. The book included instructions to the dead on how to navigate the afterlife, from funeral planning to everything that happened afterwards. And you can't get much more optimistic than that.

She added, "Having agnostic beliefs feels optimistic and safe, I think. I don't know anything but the reality that is in front of me, so I will deal with that for now. And when I die, if all ceases to exist for me, then good. That is okay. It won't be okay for those I leave behind, but they will eventually move past it. An afterlife seems scary, because many people describe it as a continuance, like they will be granted extra time to live in another form. If this so, will they have the same fears and concerns and problems? Will married couples meet up in heaven to continue fighting about the same irreconcilable differences? Will feuding gang members continue feuding in the afterlife? Will people with opposite religious beliefs carry on wars in the afterlife and recruit people into their churches?

"The way I see it, everything has to end so that new things can begin. Humans have to die and go away, not be recycled or granted extra time to remain up to their same old habits."

OPEN INVITATION

One of the most positive responses to most surveys and polls involving the afterlife, also reflected in our survey, is that most people believe they—and almost everyone they know—are going to heaven. Fewer Americans than ever believe in hell, and most of our respondents don't even think hell is an option for most people.

They also believe that people with different afterlife beliefs will also be part of the afterlife.

"I do feel that the road of life guides us all to the same place," said John Bear Mitchell. "I don't know if it's going to take us to the place I was taught about, but I do believe we will all be a part of it in one form or another. No gates, no pearly roads, but instead, a valley where we can dance with our past and sing with the future."

"Whatever there is, we are all going there," said Rhonda St. James, the securities compliance manager.

Brian McHugh, the funeral director, agreed. "I believe it is a big tent and those that follow the real Golden Rule—Do unto others as you would have done unto you—will be welcomed through the Pearly Gates."

HERE ON EARTH

Despite all the talk of heaven and the afterlife, it's life here on earth that our responders were most concerned about.

John Reed, the high school teacher, said his journey through life is what changed his beliefs from what he had been raised with, and the journey itself has been what it's all about.

"I was raised Catholic, and we were always told about the traditional heaven and hell. All the people I love are in heaven looking down on me, and if I misbehave, I'll burn in hell. I also grew up believing in limbo (though it was abolished before I was born) and Purgatory. I said many prayers to release people from Purgatory. But I never questioned anything until I was 14 or 15 years old."

He said, "Studying literature and writing stories of my own has led me to understand that we are a symbolic species, and we share many of our symbols across societies and times and places. I guess I'm pretty Jungian in that way, but I haven't studied him. I see so many people wish so hard for something to be true, and fall for so many tricks like Jonathan Edwards talking to the dead. The afterlife is a symbol of all our hopes, dreams, and vindictiveness, and we wish it to be real, so for many people, it is."

Now, he says, "I don't practice anything, though for a while as an adult I was an Episcopalian, and enjoyed it. But then I traveled cross-country with a friend, and met so many different kinds of people, I couldn't even do that anymore. One thing that led me to this was to see amazing rock formations and forests. I didn't become an 'outdoorsman,' but I appreciate it more than I do ritual. Bob Dylan says, 'You find God in the Church of your choice, you find Woody Guthrie in Brooklyn State Hospital . . . you find both in the Grand Canyon at sundown.'

"It's true."

Michael Hawkins, the college biology student, said, "My lack of belief in an afterlife precisely puts responsibility on me. I have no excuse other than what can be found in reality for my actions. If I am to live up to anything, it is my own morals, my own social contract. Life matters if an afterlife does not exist."

Anna Rossi said, "So much evil has been done in the name of religion." She added, "I think we should try to live a good life because it makes it better for all of us. We should treat all people with respect and our fragile earth with respect so that future generations can live here in peace. We should make our heaven here on earth. Not make it a hell."

Father Damian Milliken said the basic positive human feeling that comes with completing a task well should be what we all strive for, and what gives us pleasure in life.

"It's more about human nature—the satisfaction of a job well done," he said.

He sees that satisfaction every day in the achievements of the students at the girls' school he built in Tanzania.

"You see a little girl, five or six, walk up to a blackboard and do ten math problems, every one all in row. And you see the satisfaction of a job well done. That satisfaction can't be taken away from you. It's human nature to want a reward for a job well done and there's no reward like that sense of satisfaction."

And he said that sense of satisfaction is what should matter in life. "Is it a job well done?"

Or as Mark Henderson, who is wonderfully qualified to realize how precious time on earth is, no matter what awaits, said, "Keep going day to day. What can I accomplish today? I won't be able to accomplish much for too many days, but what can I do today?"

CONCLUSION

So there you have it—the CEO, the teacher, the sheet-metal worker, the dog sitter. The funeral director, the survivor of a deadly illness, and the former minister facing death.

They all had wildly different views, but in a sense, very similar views.

The surveys were answered, the experts weighed in, we compiled the results, mulled over the meanings. We didn't expect to have a definitive answer to what happens when we die. We didn't expect to provide you with some kind of outline, or template, to prepare for it.

As we said in the introduction, this isn't a scientific survey. But maybe you'll see yourself here. Or maybe you'll see your mom, or brother. Or maybe that person sitting next to you at the office.

And maybe it will help you understand them all a little better.

What we hoped to do was simply say this is who we are. And this is what we think about the big questions—and the biggest question of all. Because, whatever may happen, wherever we end up, no matter who we are—the priest, the rabbi, the editor, the professor, the engineer, the college student, or the bookseller—it will happen to all of us.

And that may be the one answer we can all agree on.

APPENDIX: CONTRIBUTORS AND RESOURCES

CONTRIBUTORS

John Griffin, professor and the director of Online Distance Education, World University, Ojai, California (*www.worldu.edu*). He is in the process of completing *Trip of a Lifetime*, a book of near-death experience and after-death perspectives.

Andrew Gurevich, professor of literature and philosophy, Mount Hood Community College, Gresham, Oregon.

E. Brooks Holifield, PhD, Charles Howard Candler Professor of American Church History in the Candler School of Theology and the Graduate Division of Religion at Emory University, specializing in religious history, the history of Christian thought in America, and early colonial American religion. He has written numerous books and articles and lectured widely on themes in American religious history.

Jeffrey Long, MD, author of *Evidence of the Afterlife*, *www.nderf.org*.

Franny Syufy, cat expert and blogger, *http://cats.about.com*.

RESOURCES

The following articles, books, and websites were incredibly helpful in compiling the information for this book. They are loaded with lots of interesting information and are highly recommended for further reading on the topic of an afterlife.

Catholic Online: *www.catholiconline.org*

Cremation Solutions: *www.cremationsolutions.com*

Fitzpatrick, Laura, "Is There Such a Thing as Life After Death?" (January 22, 2010, *Time*) *www.time.com/time/health/article/0,8599,1955636,00.html*

Goelet, Ogden Jr., "Egyptian Book of the Dead" (*www.death reference.com*)

Gray, Helen T., "Do Pets Await Masters in the Afterlife?" (August 21, 2008, *Kansas City Star*)

Harris polls (*www.harrisinteractive.com/vault/Harris-Interactive-Poll-Research-The-Religious-and-Other-Beliefs-of-Americans-2003-2003-02.pdf*)

The Internet Movie Database: *www.IMDb.com*, *All Dogs Go to Heaven*

Kerby, Rob, "So, Stephen Hawking Doesn't Expect to Go to Heaven?" (May 16, 2011, *www.blog.beliefnet.com*)

Koppen, Jean and Anderson, Gretchen, "Thoughts on the After-life Among U.S. Adults 50+" (June 2007, *AARP The Magazine*, *www.aarp.org*)

MacLaine, Shirley (*www.shirleymaclaine.com*)

Merkin, Daphne, "In Search of the Skeptical, Hopeful, Mystical Jew That Could Be Me" (April 13, 2008, *New York Times Magazine*, *www.nytimes.com*)

McCombs, Terry, "Afterlives" (*www.spiralnature.com*)

Ojimwa, "The Meriam Report" (*www.nativeamericannetroots.net*)

Paulson, Michael, "What Lies Beneath" (June 29, 2008, *The Boston Globe*, *www.boston.com/bostonglobe/ideas/articles/2008/06/29/what_lies_beneath/*)

Pew Forum on Religion and Public Life, U.S. Religious Landscape Survey (*http://religions.pewforum.org/reports*)

Pew Forum on the Future of the Global Muslim Population (*http://pewforum.org/The-Future-of-the-Global-Muslim-Population.aspx*)

Religion News Service, "Poll Says Pets Might Go to Heaven, Even if You Might Not" (2006 Washington Post poll, *www.thefreelibrary.com*)

Research America, "Top Concerns About Aging: Failing Health, Mental Ability" (February 6, 2006, *www.researchamerica.org*)

Roller, Julia, "Native and Christian: A Look at Christianity on Indian Reservations" *http://journalism.berkeley.edu/projects/nm/julia/titlepage.html*

Sample, Ian, "Stephen Hawking: 'There is No Heaven: It's a Fairy Story'" (May 15, 2011, guardian.co.uk) and "Gods of Science: Stephen Hawking and Brian Cox Discuss Mind Over Matter" (Sept. 11, 2010, *www.guardian.co.uk*)

Saxton, Bryon, "Do You Believe in Ghosts?" (April 27, 2011, *Standard Examiner, www.standard.net/topics/ghosts*)

Shouler, Ken, *The Everything® World's Religions Book, Vol. II* (Adams Media, 2009)

Spitz, Elie Kaplan, "Do Jews Believe in the Soul's Survival?" (Jewish Light Publishing, 2002)

Sussman, Dalia, "See Spot Go to Heaven? The Public's Not So Sure" (ABC News/Beliefnet poll, 2001, *www.beliefnet.com*)

Syufy, Franny, "Quest for the Rainbow Bridge" (*http://cats.about.com/od/lossandgrieving/a/rainbowbridge.htm*)

Valea, Ernest, "Reincarnation, Its Meaning and Consequences" (*www.comparativereligion.com*)

INDEX

Pets, 113–23

Plato, 39

Platonism, 75

Pluto, 5

Polytheistic religions, 6

Pre-Christian views, 4–8

Predestination, 9, 10

Presbyterians, 9

Protestants, 9–11, 122

Prothero, Stephen, 76

Pseudo-science, 65

Purgatory, 21, 26–28

Puritans, 9–10

Ra, 4

Rainbow Bridge, 113, 116–20

Rebirth, 35

Reed, John, xxi, 18, 27–28,
  91–92, 109–10, 121, 125, 134,
  144, 167, 176, 185, 190

Reincarnation, 6, 33, 75

  believers in, 40–42

  history of belief in, 38–39

  lack of belief in, 44–46

  popularity of, 36–38

views of, 42–44

Religion. *See also* Organized
  religion; *specific religions*

  African, 8, 47–48, 55–61

  afterlife and, 11–12

  Eastern, 6–7, 33–36, 95

  polytheistic, 6

  rejection of organized, x

Religious beliefs, ix

Republicans, 101

Resomation, 142

Resurrection, 64

Revelation, 21–22

Robidoux, Jim, xxi, 45–46,
  86–87, 90, 111, 120, 133, 171,
  174, 180–81, 186

Roller, Julia, 53–54

Romans, 3, 5

Rossi, Anna, xxi, 14, 26, 32, 42, 116,
  127, 133, 143, 177, 180, 187, 191

Sagan, Carl, 181

Scattergood, Martin, xxi, 18,
  46, 87–88, 122, 134, 142–43,
  157–58, 170–71, 181

Schmeidler, John, 122

Schneider, Ilene, xii, xxi–xxii, 23, 29, 45, 69, 82, 92, 109, 121, 134, 138–39, 166–67, 173

Science, 165–72

Scientology, 67

Scopes Monkey Trial, 84

Secular humanism, 12, 68

Segal, Alan F., 11

Shangdi, 7

Shouler, Ken, xxii, 14, 34, 35, 38–39, 41, 47, 49–50, 55–58, 65, 66, 82, 87, 108–09, 134, 173, 181

Sife, Wallace, 117

Sisyphus, 5

Skeptics, 81–96

Soul

immortality of, 24, 64

Jewish belief of, 8, 28

Spiritism, 68

Spirits, 97–105, 108–11

Spiritualism, 68

Spitz, Elie Kaplan, 8, 28

St. James, Rhonda, xxii, 16, 31–32, 39, 109, 115, 154, 175, 188–89

Syufy, Franny, 116–18, 143

Tantalus, 5

Taoism, 38

Terminal illness, 152–54, 158–64

Terry, Kim, 98

Time, 40

Tomoanchan, 6

Torah, 8, 28

Transmigration, 35

Tribal beliefs, 47–61

Twain, Mark, 48

Underworld, 5–6

U.S. Religion Landscape Survey, x

Utah, 98

Valea, Ernest, 36, 38

Vermont, 10

Vinyardi, Jack, 114–15

ABOUT THE AUTHOR

Maureen Milliken is a writer, journalist, and editor who lives in central Maine. She blogs about social issue and things in the news at *www.somethingoingonhere.blogspot.com*. Her website is *www.maureenmilliken.com*.

BEYOND HERE

Sure, this world is fascinating, but *what's beyond is even more intriguing...*

Want a place to share stories and experiences about all things strange and unusual? From UFOs and apparitions to dream interpretation, the Tarot, astrology, and more, the **BEYOND HERE** blog is the newest hot spot for paranormal activity!

Sign up for our newsletter at
www.adamsmedia.com/blog/paranormal
and download our free Haunted U.S. Hot Spots Map!